To Peter

My complements

Confederately your

Colonel Blue Jack

Travis

1/16/13

3

MEN OF GOD, ANGELS OF DEATH

HISTORY OF THE ROWAN ARTILLERY

MAJOR JAMES REILLY OF WILMINGTON, NORTH CAROLINA
CAPTAIN JOHN A. RAMSAY OF SALISBURY, NORTH CAROLINA

BY JACK TRAVIS

WWW.COLBLACKJACKTRAVIS.COM

www.colblackjacktravis.com

TABLE OF CONTENTS

ACKNOWLEDGMENTS

Throughout my research, I have been fortunate to enjoy the friendship and assistance of Captain Ramsay's great-grandson, John E. Ramsay of Raleigh, North Carolina, and the great-grandson of Major Reilly, James Reilly Lee, M.D., of Islamorada, Florida. I am also thankful for the help of David Moore, D.V.M., of Blacksburg, Virginia, great-grandson of Captain E. Lewis Moore.

I owe a deep debt of gratitude to my friend and fellow reenactor, Jim (Boo) McKee, historian at the North Carolina Maritime Museum in Southport, North Carolina. His tireless efforts in obtaining obscure facts and locating rare books were of great value to my research.

My appreciation goes out to my old friend and fellow reenactor, Major James Mills, surgeon of Alexander's Field Hospital, from Thomasville, North Carolina. Others who furnished assistance include Wayne Carver, Bob Cooke and Chris E. Fonvielle, Ph.D., all valuable members of the Cape Fear Civil War Round Table of Wilmington, North Carolina, and to Ed and Susan Curtis of Salisbury, North Carolina and Henry Mintz of Western North Carolina.

As always, I am very thankful for the friendship and continued encouragement of Justine Lerch of Wilmington, North Carolina.

I am very appreciative to the following, whose help greatly aided in the completion and creation of this manuscript:

Susan Lintelmann, Manuscripts Curator, United States Military Academy, West Point, New York; B. D. Patterson, Ph.D., Confederate Research Center, Hillsboro, Texas; Jane Yates, Director, The Citadel Memorial Museum of Charleston, South Carolina; Jessica Tyree, Research Assistant, Southern Historical Collection, Wilson Library, University of North Carolina at Chapel Hill; William A. Montgomery, Reference Librarian, Atlanta-Fulton Public Library; Venita Boyd, All Saints Episcopal Church, Sharon Chapel of Alexandria, Virginia; Hilda Bradberry, Headquarters Library of the United Daughters of the Confederacy, Richmond, Virginia; Jan Durden, President of the Georgia Division of the United Daughters of the Confederacy, Atlanta, Georgia; Erica Danylchak, Research Associate, Atlanta History Center Archives, Atlanta, Georgia; Thomas Lanham, Assistant Registrar, Louisiana State Museum, New Orleans, Louisiana; Bill Stafford, Louisiana State Archives, Baton Rouge, Louisiana; Lib Taylor, Rowan County Public Library, Salisbury, North Carolina; Beverly Tatterton, State and Local History Librarian, New Hanover Public Library, Wilmington, North Carolina.

Thank you to my editors, and new friends, Rodney Dillon and Barbara Poleo of Past Perfect Florida History, Inc., for their dedication to the successful completion of this book.

Special recognition and thank you to the individuals who assisted me at the following historic sites:

David Jurgella and Al Preston, Historians, South Mountain State Park, Boonsboro, Maryland; Ted Alexander, Historian, Antietam National Battlefield, Sharpsburg, Maryland; Chris Clarkins, Historian, Petersburg National Battlefield, Petersburg, Virginia; Robert Krick, Jr., Historian, Richmond National Battlefield, Richmond, Virginia; Stacy Humphreys, Historian, Fredericksburg & Spotsylvania National Military Park, Fredericksburg, Virginia ; Ray Flowers, Historian, Fort Fisher North Carolina State Historic Site, Wilmington, North Carolina.

To anyone whom I might have inadvertently forgotten, I express my sincere thanks.

Dedicated To The Loving Memory Of
Susan Bohigian
September 6, 1923 — August 31, 1987
"My Sweet Little Auntie Sue"

INTRODUCTION

One bright and sunny day over twenty-five years ago, I found myself at the Travis Cemetery in rural St. Helena Parish, Louisiana. My Aunt Sheila DeArmond had taken me to the family burial ground for the first time. As I stood staring at one of the many headstones that particularly interested me, that of Barret Travis… "Black Barret," I asked who he was. My aunt replied, "That's your great-great grandfather, a Confederate soldier in the War Between the States." He had a special talent for working with gunpowder to blow up Yankee supply boats along the many waterways of Louisiana, hence the name "Black Barret." At that moment something strange and inexplicable hit me like a bolt of lightning. It started what would become an insatiable desire to learn all I could about my genealogy and that particular time in American history.

My genealogical research gave me proof of family history beyond my wildest imagination. The family tree encompasses De La Travers, a knight chieftain who came to England with William the Conqueror in 1066, Edward Travis, who settled in Jamestown, Virginia in 1620, and Colonel William Barret Travis of Saluda, South Carolina, who gave his life for Texas independence in the defense of the Alamo in 1836. In addition, I documented over seven Confederate soldiers from the rank of a brigadier general to that of the common soldier.

This research allowed me to join several heritage groups from the Sons of Confederate Veterans and Military Order of the Stars and Bars to the Sons of the American Revolution. I could not gain enough knowledge to quench my thirst for the history of the War Between the States. I started by organizing a small Civil War battle reenactment in Wake Forest, North Carolina, which gave me a great respect for reenactors of both the Union and Confederate sides.

Naturally, the next step was to try my hand at reenacting. One of my first events was the Battle of Secessionville held at Boone Hall Plantation outside Charleston. I was able to help crew on an artillery piece and I "saw the elephant." At this event I also bonded with two other Confederate reenactors and we decided to form our own North Carolina artillery unit. In 1995 Cliff "Cannonball" Lewis and Mike "Stump" Vance, along with me, "Black Jack," formed the Tenth North Carolina Company D First North Carolina Artillery or Reilly's Battery. This unit was chosen because of its most outstanding record and performance with the Army of Northern Virginia.

To gain greater access to the mega events, the unit decided to join the prestigious "Longstreet's Corps," which was also historically correct and professional. In 1996 I was appointed Chief of Artillery by General Hillsman for the corps and thus formed Alexander's Battalion with the help of my very capable Adjutant Larry Pittman. We experienced an excellent growth rate and by the time I retired from reenacting in 2004, several other professional reenactment artillery units totaling twenty-five guns had joined the battalion. Being in command of Confederate artillery at the 140th Sharpsburg and the 140th Gettysburg reenactments provided a once in a lifetime experience to control over seventy-five guns. This was as close to the real thing as one could get. I learned what battlefield confusion was really like, how to handle the wants and needs of over one thousand five hundred Confederate reenactors, how to tolerate the July heat in a wool uniform, and, most of all, how to handle all those sensitive egos of the many Confederate officers. No amount of reading, research or study can provide the tremendous amount of knowledge gleaned from actual hands-on experience.

Through the years, I collected vast amounts of materials on Reilly's/Ramsay's Battery from friends, historians, descendants, family notes, letters, official records and years of personal research. I feared that if a book was not written, the history of this premier and dedicated North Carolina artillery unit could very well be lost to future generations. I set my task to honor these brave, gallant and Christian soldiers, telling their story with a manuscript to inform the reader about its commanding officers, how the unit was founded, and the overwhelming hardships these men had to endure to defend Southern independence.

The following pages are written from a reenactor's point of view. Who better to fully understand with all his God-given senses the true feeling of war and what a battle was really like? Except for the actual experience of battle, a reenactor acquires the true gut feeling of the Civil War soldier. This knowledgeable experience will give the reader a refreshing and realistic view of the war, providing a human perspective into the realities of operating a Confederate artillery battery in the Army of Northern Virginia.

CHAPTER I

SHAMROCKS AND KILTS TO SECESSION

In their wildest dreams, James O. Reilly and his wife, Ann Brady, never expected that their son, James, would become a Confederate hero and part of American history. Born April 4, 1822 in Ballydonagh near Athlone, Ireland, James Reilly and his five siblings grew up in a traditional Irish household.

Although approximately four miles east of bustling Athlone, with its imposing castle, Ballydonagh occupied a largely rural area of County Westmeath in central Ireland. The native Gaelic language was still often heard in this region during the early nineteenth century, although English was becoming increasingly common. By the time of James Reilly's birth, the Kingdom of Ireland had been administratively merged with that of Great Britain under the Act of Union for twenty-two years.

Active resistance to the British crown had subsided, at least temporarily, but most Irishmen recognized that the so-called "Union" offered little difference from previous years of English occupation and exploitation. Most notably, a series of laws sharply restricted Irish Catholics, such as the Reillys, from freely and openly practicing their faith. During the 1820s, Irish nationalists led by lawyer and statesman Daniel O'Connell concentrated their efforts on overturning these laws. In 1829, this campaign resulted in the British parliament's passage of the Catholic Relief Act, removing most of the hated restrictions.

Land reforms moved much more slowly. Much of the Irish countryside was owned by absentee English landlords, and leased to native farmers. The difficulties this situation created for Irish tenants were aggravated by periodic potato blights, which plagued many locales during the 1820s and 1830s before erupting into a nationwide famine in the mid-1840s.

From childhood on, the idea of becoming a soldier consumed Reilly. Even though occupied Ireland had no military, this desire burned deep within until he turned sixteen. After the death of his father, and without his mother's knowledge, the boy joined the armed forces of the detested British. Fortunately, because of Reilly's youth, his mother had the option to buy his release, which she did happily and in short order.

But young Reilly had other plans. A trim man of medium height with dark hair and blue eyes, at eighteen he wasted no time in rejoining the British army. Young Reilly's actions probably caused considerable gossip and anger among his neighbors and extended family. British military forces had been hated as foreign conquerors since the first invading forces landed in the twelfth century. Nowhere did resentment of the "strangers" run deeper than in the vicinity of Athlone, site of numerous battles against the English from Medieval times to the Jacobite War of the late seventeenth century.

Ann was furious with her bull-headed son. In spite of her protests, he was of age. Since buying his release a second time was impossible, Ann decided to take a different tack. She made up her mind to get Reilly out of Ireland, virtually under the noses of British authorities.

Although Reilly resisted his mother's fierce temper and granite determination, he eventually surrendered. Following Ann's orders, he disguised himself in feminine apparel and boarded a ship bound for New York. From there he proceeded to New Jersey and took up permanent residence with an uncle. Reilly took easily to the American way of life and after five years, his acclimation was complete. He was an American.

Neither civilian life nor fear of his mother quelled his longing for military life. This passion possessed his mind and heart. The growing swell of saber-rattling, which characterized the 1840s, only strengthened his resolve. Disputes with Great Britain over the northwestern border with Canada, and with Mexico over the Rio Grande border, filled the newspapers as the United States aggressively expanded its continental boundaries. By the summer of 1845 Reilly had grown tired of waiting. He left his job as a laborer to enlist in the United States Army at Fort Columbus, New York, on August 21. Assigned to Company H, Second United States Artillery, he had achieved his lifelong goal. Reilly and the artillery made a perfect match, one to be validated again and again over the next twenty years.

Soon after enlistment, Reilly and his fellow soldiers headed for Fort Adams, Rhode Island, where they spent the winter of 1845-1846. While Reilly bided his time on garrison duty in Rhode Island, events moved rapidly on the southwestern frontier. The border between the new state of Texas and Mexico had long been contested. The United States government insisted that the boundary followed the Rio Grande River, while the government of Mexico claimed that it corresponded with the Nueces River to the north. American expansionists, including President James K. Polk, also made no secret of their desire to acquire the Mexican states of California and New Mexico, which heightened tensions between the two countries. In January, President Polk ordered an army commanded by General Zachary Taylor to advance across the Nueces into the disputed territory. When Mexican troops crossed the Rio Grande, war seemed imminent.

During the spring, Company H received orders to return to Fort Columbus, where they embarked on a transport ship for Port Isabel, Texas. Fighting had broken out on April 24, when a Mexican cavalry force ambushed a small detachment of dragoons from Taylor's army. When the company arrived in early May, they learned that Taylor had defeated larger Mexican forces at Palo Alto and Resaca de Palma a few days earlier. On May 13, 1846, Congress officially declared war. Reilly and the rest of Company H traveled by steamer up the Rio Grande to Reynosa, where they spent the remainder of the year. Their principle opposition came not from the regular Mexican army, but from guerrilla attacks by the local rancheros.

In 1847, the company returned to the mouth of the Rio Grande, at Brazos Santiago, to join the large army being assembled there by General Winfield Scott (Old Fuss & Feathers). Here, Reilly volunteered for service with Light Battery A, and accompanied his new unit on a storm-tossed voyage down the Gulf to Vera Cruz, landing point for Scott's planned advance on Mexico City.

During the march towards Mexico City, command of Battery A shifted when Lieutenant James Duncan was promoted and Lieutenant Henry J. Hunt, a Detroit, Michigan native and graduate of West Point Class of 1839, assumed command. Reilly later vividly recalled the extreme heat and dry conditions which the army suffered along the way.

After participating in the Battle of Cerro Gordo in April, Battery A, along with the rest of Scott's army, camped for several months at Puebla. Here, Scott hoped, his troops could avoid long marches during the height of the blistering summer, receive reinforcements, and rest in preparation for the final assault on the Mexican capital. Instead, the army fell victim to diarrhea and dysentery, which Reilly attributed to "impure water and too much fresh pork." Reilly himself became so seriously ill that he could not mount a horse. On August 1, Company A was ordered to Humantla, but Reilly and several other ailing artillerymen were told to report to the hospital in Puebla. They appealed to their former lieutenant,

Brevet Lieutenant Colonel Duncan, who reluctantly allowed them to go with the company. Reilly credited this expedition with saving his life, adding that he was not sick again during the rest of his tour in Mexico.

On August 10, a few days after Company A returned to Puebla, the entire army resumed their march. "It was a welcome day to all," Reilly later wrote, "when the command 'Forward' was given, and we set out for the City of the Aztecs."

By mid-August 1847, Battery A reached the outskirts of the town of Churubusco, near a long causeway bordered by swamps. As the American column approached the causeway, the Mexican artillery opened fire with a shower of shot and shell. Battery A took cover in a natural shelter until Hunt ordered them to cross with two guns and flank the Mexican position, a chapel, housing riflemen and cannoneers manning heavy artillery pieces. Soldiers on battery horses galloped furiously along the causeway under heavy fire and worked their way behind the enemy position, where they unlimbered both guns and delivered an astonishing rate of fire into both the Mexicans and the church. The rate of exchange mounted until Mexican resistance finally crumbled. The men of Battery A then turned their attention to their wounded, including Reilly, who had sustained severe injuries to several parts of his body.

On September 14, 1847, United States forces captured Mexico City. The wounded troops, Reilly among them, were transferred to Tacubaya for medical treatment and convalescence. Reilly remained there until the early summer of 1848, drawing strength and healing from the balmy climate, the orange groves, ripe fruit, and hummingbirds.

In June 1848, as a reward for his bravery and his fine showing in battle, Reilly won appointment to orderly-sergeant of Battery A, United States Artillery. Hunt, who had earned a promotion to captain, departed with Battery A for New Orleans. On arrival he was notified that his battery, as well as three others, would lose their horses as a result of War Department cutbacks, rendering them a mounted unit in name only. With no options left, the battery headed back to Fort Columbus.

Reilly returned to Fort Columbus with Battery A, just as his term of enlistment drew to a close. On July 19, 1848, he married Ann Quinn from Ireland, ten years his junior, at St. Paul's Roman Catholic Church in Brooklyn with Reverend J. A. Schmeller officiating and witnessed by Patrick Corran and Catharine Byrms. Still, his love for military life prevailed over affection for his young bride. Scarcely three weeks after his trip to the altar, Reilly reenlisted at Fort Columbus on August 7, 1848. The couple would spend the next twelve years going from post to post by covered wagon. The birthplaces of their children tell the story of their travels across America with the United States Army.

The loss of Battery A's horses was only the beginning of the War Department's process of downsizing. After the war with Mexico, Battery A was dissolved, and Hunt and Reilly were transferred to Battery M of the Second United States Artillery. Reilly joined his new command in Charleston, South Carolina, where he was stationed in and around Fort Moultrie. During their stay, Ann bore two children, John William on April 27, 1851, and Mary Ann on February 13, 1853. The Reilly family loved Charleston and reveled in the kindness and courtly manners of their southern neighbors. But they also observed firsthand the machinations of southern politics and the sectionalism that grew more defined day by day. They recognized the social, cultural, and political differences in their newly formed social circles.

Summer of 1853 saw Charleston raging with a yellow fever outbreak and southern political differences with the North growing ever stronger. Orders from Washington had arrived for Battery M to make its way to Fort Washita, Indian Territory, in what is now Oklahoma. This journey was long and arduous, particularly for Reilly's family, who traveled alongside the battery. They did, however, stop at Fort Smith, Arkansas, to rest and pick up horses, cannons, limbers, carriages and a traveling forge. But when they reached Fort Washita, they made a shocking discovery. The fort was in shambles.

Hunt was furious that Jefferson Davis, Secretary of the War Department, had sent the battery out to a dilapidated outpost without warning them of its condition. This event set in motion Hunt and Reilly's lifelong dislike for Davis, which intensified as the war clouds gathered.

For the present though, Hunt and Reilly put aside their anger and set to work rebuilding the fort. With everything finally in order, the men now concentrated on a new drill system. Created and designed by Hunt, this new drill manual would have far-reaching influences on artillery tactics and training in armies all over the world. To his good fortune, Reilly now had the opportunity to be one of the first instructors to teach the configuration to the army's artillerymen. At Fort Washita, Hunt received friends and fellow officers, including Robert E. Lee, Joseph E. Johnston, Armistead Long and Braxton Bragg, who came to study artillery tactics under his tutelage. This foreshadowed the gathering of the angels of death.

One day on patrol, Reilly saw smoke in the distance. It could only mean one thing, an Indian attack. As the patrol drew nearer, they found the remains of a wagon train. The warring Indians had burned the wagons and apparently killed everyone.

Suddenly, from the underbrush, they heard a young girl weeping. The sole survivor from the raid, she told her rescuers that the Indians had slaughtered her entire family. The child's plight so moved Reilly that he took her back to the fort, where she became part of his growing family. Though the story has all the markings of legend, hard facts document its authenticity, at least in part. The 1860 Census of Brunswick County, North Carolina lists a Frances M. Reilly, female, age thirteen years. Unfortunately she has disappeared into the mists of history.

On April 19, 1856 another child, Delia, was born to the growing Reilly family, but her life would be tragically short. As 1856 drew to a close, Battery M was again unhorsed and sent from Fort Washita to Fort Monroe, Virginia, where on February 13, 1857, Delia died and was buried, only nine months after her birth.

Shortly afterward, Reilly was ordered to Fort Myers, Florida for seacoast and garrison service. Unbeknownst to him, he would not see his old artillery commander, Hunt, until after southern independence was declared, when they faced each other as enemies across battlefields.

While on duty at Fort Myers, Reilly received an appointment to ordnance sergeant, but the stay was not entirely peaceful. Fort Myers was one of many army posts in Florida active in the third and final war between the United States and the Seminole Indians. The hostilities, which began in the 1810s, when Florida was still a Spanish territory, consisted of long periods of uneasy truce and intermittent violence, punctuated by three periods of open warfare. The First Seminole War, an outgrowth of the Creek Wars in Georgia and Alabama, erupted in 1817, when United States forces invaded Spanish Florida in pursuit of Seminole raiding parties who had attacked American homesteads, carrying away livestock, goods and slaves. Andrew Jackson, already a veteran Indian fighter and hero of the War of 1812, destroyed Indian villages between the Apalachicola and Suwannee Rivers, and eventually captured Spanish Pensacola, igniting an international incident which led the United States to purchase Florida.

By the 1830s, when Andy Jackson (Old Hickory), now president of the United States, called for the removal of southeastern Indians to unsettled lands west of the Mississippi River, tensions between the Seminoles and the United States government again reached the breaking point. The Second Seminole War, which began in 1835, raged across Florida and lasted seven years. The United States Army and Navy, as well as militia units from several southeastern states, captured and removed large numbers of Florida Indians and eventually drove the remnant deep into the Everglades and Big Cypress Swamp at the southern end of the territory. The final phase of the war centered on amphibious operations designed to flush out the elusive Seminoles. In 1842 with public opposition mounting, especially in the North, and funding diminishing, the United States declared the war over and defined the boundaries of a reservation in southwest Florida for the small groups of remaining Indians.

By the 1850s, a series of Seminole raids on white settlements, coupled with growing pressure to reclaim and settle the south Florida wilderness, led to renewed calls for complete Indian removal. After a series of futile negotiations with Seminole leaders, United States troops and surveying parties entered the reservation, hoping to pressure the remaining bands to emigrate. In December 1855, Seminoles led by Billy Bowlegs attacked an army patrol in the Big Cypress Swamp, igniting the Third Seminole War. For the next three years troops endeavored to protect isolated settlements from Indian attacks and penetrate the Big Cypress and Everglades in search of hostile Seminoles. Fort Myers on the Caloosahatchee River offered access to both the Big Cypress and the Gulf of Mexico and served as a center of military operations in southwest Florida throughout the war.

While troops penetrated the Florida wilderness in an attempt to round up the last remnants of the Seminoles for transport to reservations in the West, an effort never entirely successful, Reilly managed to befriend several friendly Seminoles. So affectionate was the relationship that when his daughter, Sue, was born on December 30, 1858, the Seminoles called her "Little White Papoose." Legend has it that a Seminole chief, fascinated with the baby's blue eyes and blond hair, wanted to buy her. Reilly would have no part of that and gracefully declined the offer.

By 1859 the Third Seminole War had come to an inconclusive end and the Reilly family was back in Charleston. As an ordnance sergeant, Reilly served at the Charleston Arsenal, located within the city limits, right in the heart of fire-breathing secessionist sentiment. Feelings ran deep and tempers blazed. By this time many southerners wanted to be free, independent and out of the Union. They hated the Yankee North and viewed that culture as greed-driven. Nowhere in the South were these sentiments more powerful than in Charleston.

Reilly knew war was very close and he struggled with the implications. What would he do? Which side would he support? Did his loyalties lie with the Union or with the South? These questions baffled him.

In 1860 Reilly and his family transferred to Fort Johnston in the town of Smithville, now Southport, North Carolina, at the mouth of the Cape Fear River.

Settlers had founded the fort in colonial days to guard the waterway's entrance. During Reilly's tour of duty, the fort was little more than a barracks. Even so, he was responsible for the ordnance and the general well-being of the stronghold and everyone within its walls.

The Reilly clan continued to flourish. A son, Thomas Owen, was born at Fort Johnston on April 17, 1860. This happy event only enhanced the family's enjoyment of this peaceful small town. But forces were in play that would soon change Reilly's life, and that of the nation.

Abraham Lincoln, dubbed "Gorilla Abe" by many southerners, was elected president of the United States in November. Lincoln belonged to the newly-formed Republican Party, hated in the South because of its stance on slavery and the threat of its interference with the South's economy and lifestyle.

So, on December 20, 1860, South Carolina seceded from the Union, arguably a legal move under the United States Constitution. The people of Charleston were ecstatic. They celebrated the new state of independence to the chiming of church bells. Secession parties and mock hangings and burnings of "Gorilla Abe" erupted all over town. Citizens hung South Carolina state flags of all sizes from porches and doorways of homes, state buildings and businesses.

The festivities were both grand and premature. Little did the joyful South Carolinian secessionists know that their new independence would write the first chapter of a book inscribed in blood.

Fearing for the safety of his men, Major Robert Anderson, Union commander at Charleston, moved his troops from Fort Moultrie on the mainland to Fort Sumter in Charleston Harbor under cover of darkness on December 26, 1860. Before leaving Fort Moultrie, fleeing troops spiked the siege guns and torched carriages, rendering them useless to South Carolina. This aggressive action, coupled with the destruction of what South Carolinians regarded as state property, added more fuel to the firestorm of hatred aimed at the federal government and the Union.

President James Buchanan, serving out the last weeks of his term before Lincoln's inauguration in March, cautiously and unsuccessfully tried to preserve Federal authority in the South, while avoiding civil war.

In January, President Buchanan, acting on the advice of General Winfield Scott, secretly ordered a ship carrying two hundred armed troops with gunpowder and artillery shells to Charleston in an attempt to reinforce Fort Sumter. The *Star of the West*, a steam passenger liner that ran from New York to New Orleans, was the vessel of choice because it could steam directly into Charleston Harbor without arousing suspicion. But high-ranking southern sympathizers in the Federal government leaked the news and South Carolinians awaited the arrival of the *Star of the West*.

Cadets from the Charleston Citadel Military School under the command of Colonel John Luther Branch hastily constructed a siege battery, consisting of four twenty-four pound seacoast guns. They then waited anxiously at Cummings Point on Morris Island, an excellent artillery position to block the *Star of the West* from entering the harbor. The owners of Morris Island, the Vincent family, gave the cadets a red palmetto flag, which they proudly flew from their battery. South Carolina did not adopt the navy blue palmetto state flag until late January 1861. At seven fifteen in the morning on January 9, 1861, the cadets sighted the *Star of the West* in the early morning light. Aboard ship, Lieutenant Charles J. Woods kept the men of the 9th U.S. Infantry below deck while he studied the Morris Island shore. The Citadel battery was not visible. Nonetheless, Captain John McGowan, the ship's commander, was apprehensive about his vessel. Fitted with neither guns nor armor, the *Star of the West* was not built for war.

On the island preparations were underway. Cadets loaded their guns under the battery command of Major J. M. Stevens. Captain John Marshall Whilden gave the order to fire gun Number One. Cadet George E. Haynesworth pulled the lanyard. Thus, the first shot of the war was fired at the *Star of the West*. Stunned, the Yankee troops aboard realized they were no match for the Citadel cadet battery; the ship returned to her home port, unable to deliver her ammunition and invading troops.

The *Star of the West* incident heightened fears of a Federal invasion along the coast. Armed citizens appeared at Reilly's door in Smithville, North Carolina, demanding the key to Fort Johnston's powder magazine. Reilly, as commander of the fort, an experienced army sergeant and an Irishman at that, flatly refused. The panicked townspeople informed him that if he did not surrender the keys, they would break in. Realizing that his tiny garrison was far outnumbered, Reilly shrewdly promised to relinquish the keys, if the citizens' leader provided a receipt. This accomplished, another group of activists headed to Fort Caswell, under the command of Ordnance Sergeant Frederick Dardingkiller, and achieved the same results.

Recognizing the gravity of the situation, Reilly tried to warn Washington by telegraph. To do this he needed to reach Wilmington, but the most expedient route was by water, the armed citizens had control of the public vessel, and no one in Smithville would provide a boat. Fortunately, the crisis was short-lived.

While the citizenry held two forts, they had no idea what to do with them. With no other support available and no Federal invasion ships in sight, they returned the keys to the forts to Reilly and Dardingkiller, the day after they commandeered them.

With the return of both forts to Federal hands, the affair appeared over. However, in the afternoon of January 10, 1861, a group of Wilmington volunteers, known as the Cape Fear Minutemen and commanded by John J. Hedrick, arrived at Smithville. Reinforced by other recruits, they advanced on and reoccupied Fort Caswell. When Governor Ellis received news of this seizure, he pronounced it to be without legal basis and ordered the fort returned to Federal authorities on January 14. The Cape Fear Minutemen evacuated Fort Caswell, ending the tense situation for the time being.

Southern citizens now had no doubts that war was inevitable. The states of the lower South rushed to hold conventions to vote on leaving the Union. By early February 1861, six additional states had seceded – Mississippi, Florida, Alabama, Georgia, Louisiana and Texas. On February 9, at the Confederate States Convention in Montgomery, Alabama, the Confederate States of America were born, with Jefferson Davis elected president and Alexander Stephens, vice president.

Reilly recognized it would only be a matter of time before North Carolina joined her sister states. In fact, Governor John W. Ellis and his government had already quietly begun to prepare for war. Still, North Carolina would be slow in seceding because its citizens were divided. Advocates of secession feared that if they did not move soon, the Federal government would reinforce the garrisons at Fort Johnston and Fort Caswell, allowing the Yankees to control the Cape Fear River, as well as the highly valuable port of Wilmington.

Along the Cape Fear River, the next few months were filled with uncertainty and anticipation. Secession and war with the "damn Yankees" were certainties, but when would North Carolina leave the Union? Many found the indecision unbearable.

The dilemma reached an abrupt resolution when Confederate forces fired on Fort Sumter the morning of April 12. After fruitless negotiation with the Federal government to remove their troops, all hope was lost. War had begun, and Virginia, Arkansas, North Carolina and Tennessee prepared to leave the Union and join the Confederacy.

When President Lincoln issued a proclamation on April 14, 1861, declaring a state of insurrection and calling for volunteers to stamp out the "rebellion," Governor Ellis telegraphed orders to Colonel Cantwell in Wilmington to take possession of Forts Caswell and Johnston in the name of the state of North Carolina. Cantwell embarked in the early morning hours of April 16 with a large body of men. He arrived at Fort Johnston about four in the afternoon. Faced with overwhelming odds, Reilly surrendered Fort Johnston under protest. Colonel Cantwell left a detachment to occupy Fort Johnston, while he proceeded to take Fort Caswell. Now, with both forts in North Carolina hands, state troops controlled the mouth of the Cape Fear River and the Port of Wilmington. On April 19, Lincoln declared a blockade of the southern coastline.

Reilly now knew he had to make the decision that had been looming for some time. Where would he pledge his allegiance? North Carolina had already seized Fort Johnston and by April 21, 1861, Reilly made his choice. He resigned from the United States Army and entered the services of North Carolina, well before the state's secession. Reilly chose to stand with the South because it was his home, where his children were born and his friends lived, and he and Ann both loved the South and its people. Reilly stood firm for the cause of southern independence and did not oppose the institution of slavery. Thus, with a heart full of newborn patriotism, he moved his family to Wilmington to prepare for war.

During this transition period, Reilly's path intersected with that of Major William H. C. Whiting, later a general, who would have a significant influence on Reilly's Confederate military career. Whiting, a Mississippian, graduated from West Point in 1845 with the highest marks ever achieved, until Douglas MacArthur of World War II fame broke his longstanding record. Whiting's arrogance, combined with his weakness for alcohol, denied him the military greatness that might have placed him alongside Lee, Jackson and Longstreet. For a brief time, Reilly served as Whiting's drillmaster in Wilmington.

On the basis of Whiting's recommendation, Governor Ellis commissioned Reilly to the rank of first lieutenant in May 1861. Lieutenant Reilly served a very short period with Company A, Tenth Regiment North Carolina State Troops, First North Carolina Artillery, known as "Ellis Flying Artillery." Later, this unit was dubbed "Manly's Battery," after Captain Basil C. Manly.

Meanwhile, Governor Ellis conceived the idea of forming a new artillery battery from the old gunless Rowan Artillery unit, commanded by Captain John A. Ramsay. Hailing from the town of Salisbury in Rowan County, Ellis was quite familiar with the leadership skills of Captain Ramsay, as well as with his popularity among his men and the people of the county. Later he used Reilly's sixteen years of United States artillery experience. As a veteran of the Mexican War, Reilly had the perfect credentials to create an outstanding North Carolina artillery battery.

In Washington, Lincoln immediately called on the states for troops to squelch the southern insurrection. After Governor John W. Ellis of North Carolina received the request, his state voted to secede from the union on May 20, 1861. For good measure, Governor Ellis sent the following reply to Washington, D.C.:

> *I regard the levy of troops made by the administration for the purpose of subjugating the states of the South as a violation of the constitution and a gross usurpation of power. I can be no party to this wicked violation of the country, and this war upon the liberties of a free people. You can get no troops from North Carolina.*

The nature of the war would be determined by each side's overall objectives and goals. Under the direction of General-in-Chief Winfield Scott, the North launched the Anaconda Plan to blockade southern ports and to gain control of the Mississippi River, like the giant snake squeezing the life blood out of the southern states by cutting vital supply lines from Europe. The Yankees also determined to invade the South, carrying on an offensive war to defeat the Confederacy and to capture its capital at Richmond, Virginia.

On the other hand, the South's strategy was essentially defensive. If invaded, the Confederate Army was prepared to do all possible to repel the Union forces. At various times during the war, Confederate leaders also considered a counterattack on Washington, D.C., hoping that capturing the Federal capital would obtain recognition of southern freedom by the Federal government. The South knew full well it did not have the manufacturing output of the North. But while primarily an agricultural plantation society, rich with King Cotton, the Confederacy put up a good fight in the hopes that the North might concede its independence.

John Andrew Ramsay, son of Robert Alexander Ramsay and Mary Walton, was born April 29, 1836 in a log cabin on the family farm in Iredell County, North Carolina. His family tree branched back to Ulster Scots, or Scots Irish, who had immigrated to the American colonies about 1730. The family traveled the Old Wagon Road to Coddle Creek Settlement, now located in Iredell County. There they built a log cabin, which became the homestead of the Ramsay family for many generations.

The Ramsays were strong-willed people, ready to fight for their freedom and independence. Many of John's ancestors fought in the American Revolution, as members of the North Carolina Continental Line. Robert and Andrew Ramsay were engaged at Ransour's Mill and Charlotte Courthouse. At the Battle of Cowpens, South Carolina, Andrew killed a British soldier who refused to surrender.

While growing up on the Ramsay farm, young John gained an interest in mathematics and engineering. As an adult, he was able to obtain a position as a surveyor, a vocation he pursued with great enthusiasm. John was a devout Presbyterian and developed an excellent reputation among the people of Iredell and Rowan Counties. These qualities proved to be invaluable assets to his future success in life.

At age twenty-two, Ramsay decided to volunteer for the new state militia unit being organized in Salisbury. On May 18, 1858, under Section 91, Chapter 70 of the Revised Code of the State of North Carolina, the unit was incorporated as the Rowan Artillery and furnished with two long guns and fifty swords.

By the spring of 1861, war was on the lips of every man in the artillery. All waited impatiently for North Carolina to secede from the Union so they could fight those "damn Yankees." Orders came on May 3 from Adjutant-General John F. Hoke to commence a twelve-month regular course of military training and drill at the old cotton factory in Salisbury. Emotions ran hot and high, for these young men wanted desperately to protect their families, homes and the southern way of life from the expected Yankee invasion. Men and women were enraptured with idealistic visions of fighting for their independence.

Men of the battery elected officers on May 8. John A. Ramsay was elected captain, Calvin M. Black became first lieutenant, and William W. Myers and Jesse F. Woodard were elected second lieutenants. These men would provide leadership and set fearless personal examples for the cannoneers to follow, both in war and in peace.

On May 23, Ramsay received orders from the adjutant-general of North Carolina for the battery to proceed to Weldon and report to the commanding officer, but the men could not arrange rail transportation before May 25. While they remained in town, the ladies of Salisbury presented a beautiful and richly-made flag to Ramsay and the Rowan Artillery on the afternoon before they departed. The flag was lovingly handmade by Miss Martha McRorie, Miss Mary Myers and Mrs. Rosa Benjamin, who made the presentation and gave a most eloquent address to the crowd of onlookers. Ramsay in turn delivered a wonderful speech in thanks, less than a minute long. To quote the *Carolina Watchman*, May 27, 1861, "He is a man of action, not words." Although there is no detailed description of the flag, it has been said that it was in the Confederate First National Flag style.

When the military transport train arrived at Salisbury on May 25, 1861, feelings ran high, as family, friends and loved ones bid them farewell. The men began their journey to Weldon, North Carolina and the unknown events that would see many killed or badly wounded over the next four years on the battlefields with the Army of Northern Virginia. At this early juncture their spirits and hopes were high with expectations for a speedy southern victory. They arrived in Weldon on May 28.

The men of the as yet gunless Rowan Artillery spent the next few weeks in Weldon, drilling and training with the Fourth Regiment, North Carolina State Troops under the command of Colonel G. B. Anderson. On June 12, Governor Ellis telegraphed Ramsay, instructing him to come to Raleigh. During this meeting, Ellis informed him that the cost of equipping the battery was too great and that he was unwilling to do so unless the battery would enlist for the duration of the war. Ramsay returned to Weldon and informed his men of the governor's request. Within a three day period, every single one enlisted for the duration.

Ramsey returned to Raleigh on June 25 to see Ellis concerning the procurement of arms and equipment. Finding the governor in very poor health, Ramsay was informed that the state still could not afford to buy cannons for the battery. Ellis said he greatly regretted this situation and, though he had put forth every effort, his attempts had been to no avail. The best he could do was supply the battery with some small arms and rifles, attaching it to an infantry regiment until he could provide the necessary equipment.

Ellis also suggested that Ramsay find a trained and experienced officer to take command of the battery and to properly drill and instruct the men in the use of artillery. He told Ramsay that he knew of just such an officer, one who had served in the United States Army for seventeen years and fought in the war with Mexico. Ellis promised to send him to the battery, if the men found the idea agreeable.

When Ramsay reached Weldon, he informed his men of the governor's proposition. They accepted and joyfully at that. On June 26, Ramsay sent a communication to Ellis officially requesting the appointment of the officer. Thus, Governor John W. Ellis's skillful manipulation worked exceptionally well in creating an outstanding battery.

Reilly arrived at Weldon on June 30 to take command of the Rowan Artillery and on July 1 the battery moved, by railroad, to Camp Hill, North Carolina, near Garysburg. On July 29, 1861, the official notice from Governor Ellis and the State Military Board appointed James Reilly, captain; John Ramsay, first lieutenant; W. W. Myers, first lieutenant; Jesse T. Woodard, second lieutenant; and William L. Saunders, second lieutenant. The battery then was temporarily attached to the Fourth Regiment Infantry, North Carolina State Troops, their former drill companions commanded of Colonel G. B. Anderson. After this temporary attachment, the battery was designated the Tenth Regiment North Carolina State Troops Company D (First North Carolina Artillery).

These two commanders with strikingly different backgrounds and personalities, formed a perfect blend, which transformed the Rowan Artillery into one of the premier artillery batteries in the Army of Northern Virginia. Captain Reilly's extensive hands-on wartime experience, coupled with his proficiency and mastery of artillery, made him an outstanding commander, known for his rough, tough style and Irish brogue. Lieutenant Ramsay, more self-contained, scholarly, cultured and refined, lacked Reilly's practical experience, but was quick to learn.

Despite their differences in personality and style, Reilly and Ramsay shared qualities of unquestionable bravery and deep spiritual values. These men of God were now prepared to become the angels of death for their belief in the southern cause.

North Carolina

AN ORDINANCE to dissolve the union between the State of North Carolina and the other States united with her, under the compact of government entitled "The Constitution of the United States."

We, the people of the State of North Carolina in convention assembled, do declare and ordain, and it is hereby declared and ordained, That the ordinance adopted by the State of North Carolina in the convention of 1789, whereby the Constitution of the United States was ratified and adopted, and also all acts and parts of acts of the General Assembly ratifying and adopting amendments to the said Constitution, are hereby repealed, rescinded, and abrogated.

We do further declare and ordain, That the union now subsisting between the State of North Carolina and the other States, under the title of the United States of America, is hereby dissolved, and that the State of North Carolina is in full possession and exercise of all those rights of sovereignty which belong and appertain to a free and independent State.

Done in convention at the city of Raleigh, this the 20th day of May, in the year of our Lord 1861, and in the eighty-fifth year of the independence of said State.

CHAPTER II

FROM THE POTOMAC TO THE PENINSULA

B y July 21, 1861, the Rowan Artillery found itself in Richmond, Virginia. As was the military custom at that time, batteries and battalions took on the name of their commanding officers, and so the Rowan Artillery became known as Reilly's Battery. The battery first encamped near the lower part of the city of Richmond, called the Rockets.

On July 25, the battery departed Richmond for Manassas, Virginia to begin a camp of instruction. The Battle of Manassas, or the "Great Yankee Skeedaddle" as it was nicknamed by the Confederates, had taken place on July 21, and had resulted in a most decisive Confederate victory. The spoils of this battle yielded a wonderful surprise for the men of Reilly's Battery. They were presented with four captured Union cannons; the men were elated to finally have their own guns, making them an operational artillery battery. Needless to say, jubilation was the order of the day.

Now, "Old Tarantula," as Captain Reilly was called by his men because of his rough, gruff, grizzly and brave demeanor, began in earnest to instruct his men in the art of artillery drill and tactics. All the skills and experience gained in the Mexican War and the Indian Wars under his old commander, Henry J. Hunt, who was now the Union Chief of Artillery, were put to use to further the Confederate cause. Captain Reilly also informed the Confederate Army commander, General Joseph E. Johnston, that four more guns, six-pound mounted but without carriages, remained at Fort Johnston, North Carolina. Reilly knew Johnston, a native of Farmville, Virginia and graduate of West Point Class of 1828, from his days at Fort Washita.

The trophy guns given to Reilly's Battery included two ten-pound Parrott rifled guns, excellent for accurate long-range firing. The battery also acquired two twelve-pound Dahlgren Howitzers. Smoothbore guns, this type of cannon was particularly suited to close-range fighting, especially against advancing infantry and cavalry. The battery had a good mix of guns that could be used with great effectiveness in a multitude of battlefield situations. A Confederate battery consisted of four to six guns, depending on availability, commanded by a captain. The unit was further divided into two gun sections, each commanded by a lieutenant. Many times during the war, sections of guns would be separated from the main battery to offer special support according to what type of gun was needed for a particular situation.

On September 16, 1861, Reilly's Battery left Camp Pickens, near Manassas, and encamped near the Braddock Road, five miles northeast of Centreville. By September 25, the Parrott gun section along with Captain Reilly, Lieutenant Myers and Lieutenant Woodard, was attached to the command of General Walker. With five days rations, this detachment marched to Flint Hill, Virginia, near the Potomac River, taking part in General Johnston's new defensive line, anchored from Leesburg on the left to the Occoquan and Potomac Rivers on the right.

The Confederates built several heavy-gun siege batteries along the many points that jutted into the Potomac. These batteries were located at Freestone Point, Cockpit Point (Possum Nose), Shipping Point (now Quantico), and Evensport. Johnston intended this span of six miles, fortified with thirty-seven heavy guns, to disrupt Federal shipping and to isolate Washington, D.C. Reilly's command left camp at Flint Hill at two in the morning on September 30. Under orders to remain silent on the march, they came into battery position on the banks of the Potomac. There they received orders to open fire. Each gun fired twenty-eight shots into a large building and a Union encampment on the opposite side of the river, a distance of fourteen hundred yards. At the first volleys, the Yankee troops, occupying the building and camp, rushed out in the wildest confusion, turned tail and ran for their lives. The bombardment greatly damaged the building as well as Yankee morale. Reilly's section of Parrott guns functioned perfectly for this type of long-range attack and gave the men excellent experience in target practice.

The Battery reunited at their new encampment at Fairfax Court House. On October 16 signal rockets fired by the Yankees caused the battery to march and encamp within a mile to the rear of Centreville. While at Centreville, they participated in an artillery review and parade along with five other batteries. Reviewing officer Colonel (later General) William Nelson Pendleton, a Virginian, had graduated fifth in his class at West Point in 1830. A fellow cadet and good friend of General Robert E. Lee, Pendleton became an ordained Episcopal minister in

1838. His administrative and organizational skills, acquired as a West Pointer and a minister, impressed the Confederate high command. A few months later Pendleton was appointed Chief of Artillery, a post that eclipsed his abilities by a wide margin. At fifty-three, he lacked the stamina and fast judgment required for effective artillery field command.

Most of General Johnston's army set up winter encampments around Centreville and Dumfries, Virginia. The men of Reilly's Battery continued their artillery drilling under the watchful eye of "Old Tarantula," and prepared their winter quarters. To the men's delight, many bundles and boxes arrived from their families and friends back home in Rowan County. The folks back home had not forgotten their "Southern Soldier Boys." All types of clothing, canned provisions, and a variety of delicacies were distributed to the members of the battery. The ladies of Salisbury and Rowan County were well organized and worked hard to acknowledge the brave and gallant men of Reilly's Battery. Their efforts were duly acknowledged with many thank you letters and expressions of appreciation from the men.

The winter of 1861-62 was very severe and the roads became impassable. The bitter cold weather and subsequent shortage of forage for the horses were only two of many difficulties for the men. General Johnston waited and watched for some movement from the Federal army. The winter encampment was a time of inactivity and weariness for the men and anxiety for the generals not knowing the next movement of the Federals, now commanded by General George B. McClellan. It was also a time for reorganization and preparation for spring campaigning. Reilly's Battery was assigned to the brigade of Brigadier General William H. C. Whiting, Reilly's old friend from Wilmington.

Early in March 1862, it became apparent that General McClellan planned to move his army either to Fredericksburg or to the Peninsula of Virginia at Yorktown. McClellan, a native of Philadelphia and graduate of West Point, Class of 1846, was hailed in the North for his abundant training and organizational skills, and for building the morale of his troops. Soon, however, his overly slow and cautious strategy would overshadow these strengths.

On March 8, 1862, Reilly's Battery left camp near Dumfries headed for the south side of the Rappahannock River, where they camped near a dam not far from Fredericksburg. On March 31, sixty new recruits arrived from Rowan County. Ten more arrived by April 6. As a rule of thumb, it took twenty-five men to keep one gun in action. With four guns now in Reilly's Battery, new recruits were badly need and warmly welcomed. On April 8, the battery began a ten-day hard march to Yorktown, where they camped two miles from the city and awaited further orders. This march confirmed rumors that the Union Army was advancing on Richmond by way of the coastal rivers to the east.

During April 1862, General McClellan assembled a force of ninety thousand men at Fort Monroe, Virginia to make an attack on Richmond via the peninsula between the York and James Rivers. His strategy was to trap the Confederates between Union gunboats ascending the rivers and the Federal army advancing up the peninsula. This combination of overwhelming infantry and large gunboats with heavy guns on both rivers was no match for the small Confederate army to hold back. If Johnston's army abandoned the peninsula completely, they would leave Richmond defenseless. Thus, the Confederate strategy was to delay and confuse the Yankees, withdraw up the James and York Rivers via the peninsula toward Richmond, while reinforcing their army, and fight only on ground where they had a defensive advantage. The first action of this campaign, the Battle of Yorktown, was nothing more than a delaying action for the Confederates, stalling for time as they moved up the peninsula to a better position to defend the capital of the Confederacy and maybe to surprise and entrap the Union army.

The Confederate forces defending Yorktown were commanded by General John Bankhead Magruder, a native of Port Royal, Virginia, who had graduated tenth in the West Point Class of 1830. Magruder commanded only eight thousand to ten thousand men to hold back and delay McClellan's army of eighty-five thousand to ninety thousand Federals and buy General Johnston time to mass troops and build defensive positions around Richmond.

The Federals might have moved up the peninsula and captured Richmond before Johnston could organize sufficient defenses had it not been for Magruder's determination. Magruder was nicknamed "The Prince," because he wore gaudy, over-embellished tailored uniforms. Known as a heavy drinker, he suffered from anxiety attacks when under stress, and spoke with a lisp, which made him the subject of disparaging jokes and remarks. However, Magruder was extremely clever and successful in keeping the Federals at bay. He bluffed the Union army into thinking he had more forces than he actually had by marching his men around and revealing the same troops at different places, as well as employing "Quaker guns," logs painted black to look like siege guns. For all his faults, Magruder turned out to be the right man for the job, using his flamboyant personality to fool General McClellan.

General Pendleton summed up the situation from the artillery perspective:

It looks very much as if we have to get back nearer Richmond before having any chance of a land battle.

On the water, or anywhere near enough to it to give scope to their heavily-armed vessels, we have no way of meeting them on terms that admit of success to us.

Their large rifle-cannon so far out-shoot anything we

Have, at least in sufficient abundance, that we cannot reply to them with any effect. . .

Some of the vessels off Yorktown throw cannon-bolts of near one hundred Pounds between three and four miles, whereas our best rifle-cannons cannot reach them at three miles.

On May 4, Reilly's Battery left camp near Yorktown under orders to guard the rear of the withdrawing army, and to be prepared for instant action. The cat and mouse game began as each time the battery prepared for action, the enemy halted, only advancing when the Confederates resumed their withdrawal. About seven miles from Yorktown, another battery had left two of their guns stuck in the mud. Captain Reilly had the two guns removed, attached to two of his caissons, and resumed the march.

On May 7, the Federal troops attempted a landing at Eltham's Landing near West Point, Virginia, in an effort to divide the Confederate forces. Colonel Stephen D. Lee of South Carolina, a distant relative of Robert E. Lee and 1854 graduate of West Point, organized a special battery of rifled guns made up of Captain Reilly's two Parrott guns and two twelve-pound Blakeleys each from Captains Bachman and Moody. He placed them on a very fine artillery position he had selected on the banks of the York River, in full view of and covering the Yankee transports. They commenced firing and within a few minutes a Federal gunboat moved in and returned fire on the Confederate battery. The first shots passed over two hundred feet above the battery, but as the Union gun crews began to reduce the elevation of their guns, the last shot passed just above the heads of the crew manning Lieutenant Ramsay's left gun. Colonel Lee commanded his gunners to cease firing and move out, an order which was promptly obeyed. Captain Reilly's section had fired thirty shots at the enemy. At the same time, the Confederate infantry had driven the enemy off the shore and back to their transports. The Battle of West Point was over. Colonel Lee continued to demonstrate bravery and leadership in the Confederate army and ultimately rose to the rank of lieutenant general.

Shortly after the Battle of West Point, the Rowan Artillery obtained new guns. Lieutenant Ramsay detailed the series of events as follows

We left West Point, Va and on May 9th 1862 encampted on the Baltimore cross-roads[,] here the battery was ordered on picket duty for the next four days. The two guns we removed from the mud on our rear guard action from Yorktown were about to come into play again. On May 13th about 10am an. Officer arrived with two pairs of horses and drivers.He demanded the two guns his order was refused angrily he road off. In about an hour he returned with a note from Gen Johnston adjutant-general, requesting that the officer commanding Reilly's Battery please give his explanation for refusing to let the two guns go. Lt Ramsay wrote a brief note reciting the facts. Soon after a courier returned with a note for Lt Ramsay stating as follows

"Please find inclosed an order on the Ordnance Officer in Richmond for two field guns {your choice} and a full supply of ammunition, harness, implements, etc. for the same, and an order on the Quartermaster's Office for all the horses, etc., needed to equip two field guns. You are hereby instructed to deliver to this Captain the two guns in your possession that he claims.

"General Johnston thanks Captain Reilly, his officers and men for their patriotism, zeal and industry manifested in transporting and taking care of the guns."

These guns and the name of the battery they belonged to, as well as the name of the captain who came to claim them, have been veiled to history.

On May 20, 1862, with General Johnston's orders in hand, Captain Reilly and Lieutenant Ramsay arrived at the Ordnance Office in Richmond to procure the two promised field guns. These two three-inch ordnance rifles made by Bellona Iron Works were called Archer guns, named after Dr. Robert Archer, the owner of the foundry. The foundry that made them, aptly named Bellona after the Roman goddess of war, was located on the James River thirteen miles up from the famous Tredegar Iron Works in Richmond. Tredegar Iron Works was without question the South's most important ironmaker, both before and during the war. One of Reilly's Battery's Bellona guns was swapped for a Union three-inch rifle at Gaines Mill and the other burst at the Battle of Gettysburg, July 2, 1863. Because of the material shortages that were already beginning to plague the Confederacy, Bellona used a poorer quality of coal and pig iron that made their guns inferior to those of the Tredegar and Federal iron works. This was the main reason for the unusual bursting of Reilly's three-inch rifle gun at Gettysburg.

By the time Reilly and Ramsay rejoined the battery, the weather was having an adverse effect on the movement of both armies. Very heavy rains for days on end rendered the roads almost impassable. Rivers, creeks and other waterways overflowed and dams broke, making the movement of men, artillery and equipment extremely stressful on both man and beast. Having advanced steadily up the Peninsula as Johnston strategically retreated, General McClellan planned to mass a large force and launch an all-out attack on Richmond. With his army backed up against the capital, General Johnston could ill afford to sit idly by and watch. He had to seize the initiative and attack, which he did at Seven Pines on May 31, 1862. The Confederate attack failed utterly. Poor execution of orders caused troop movements to go askew and falter.

To make matters worse, General Johnston received severe wounds in his shoulder and arm, which incapacitated him. Late in the day, just before sundown, General Johnston and his staff were out in an open field when a musket ball smashed into his shoulder. A few seconds later, an artillery shell fragment hit him, breaking his shoulder blade and two ribs.

On June 1, 1862, General Robert E. Lee assumed command of the Confederate Army in Virginia by order of President Jefferson Davis, considered by many scholars the best decision of his presidency. General Lee, a native Virginian, graduated second in his West Point Class of 1829, amazingly with no demerits. Now, at the ripe old age of fifty-five, he commanded the Confederate army, which he named the "Army of Northern Virginia." The perception that Lee moved cautiously led the officers and men to nickname him "Granny Lee," an assessment which would soon be disproven.

Reilly's Battery was present at the Battle of Seven Pines and came under enemy fire, but did not engage. On June 1, Lieutenant Ramsay placed his Parrott gun section in a masked position, but the Federals discovered it and opened fire. Ramsay's horse was shot out from under him by a cannonball, but he suffered no injury to his person.

With McClellan's army dangerously close to Richmond, Lee decided to engage in a series of operations to test the Federal position for vulnerable spots. His first orders detailed over two hundred officers and men to act a spies, scouts and sharpshooters. On many of these clandestine operations, small but serious actions took place. One such encounter took place on June 5, when four rifled guns from Reilly's Battery dueled with the Federals across the Chickahominy River, expending eighty rounds of ammunition. Unfortunately, the battery lost four horses.

General Lee's aggressive actions earned him the respect of his men. Colonel Joseph Ives, a cavalry colonel and aide-de-camp to President Davis, summed up the army's opinion of their new commander, "If there is one man in either army…head and shoulders above every other in audacity, it is General Lee! His name might be audacity. He will take more desperate chances and take them quicker than any other general in the country, North or South, and you will live to see it."

Lee's probing operations convinced him that the Federals must be driven back by aggressive action. Meanwhile, reinforcements were turning McClellan's army into an increasingly formidable force. Lee decided that his best chance against the larger Federal army was to create a diversion. By fooling the Federals into thinking that he was sending reinforcements to General "Stonewall" Jackson's army in the Shenandoah Valley so that Jackson could attack Washington, Lee hoped to redirect Federal troops to the valley and away from the Richmond area.

Reilly's old friend, General Whiting, was placed in charge of this diversion. He was ordered to take a portion of his division, which included Reilly's Battery and a Texas brigade commanded by General John Bell Hood up to the valley. Whiting's command left Richmond on June 13, 1862, marched to Hanover Junction, boarded the Virginia Central Railroad to Charlottesville, then continued their march on to Staunton, before turning back through Gordonsville. General Whiting became visibly frustrated with marching up the valley only to turn around and march back down. He openly criticized both Lee and Jackson, and his condescending behavior would play out to his extreme disadvantage in the coming months.

Despite Whiting's criticism, Lee's strategy proved tremendously successful. Fearful of an attack on Washington, McClellan sent reinforcements from his army to help protect the capital. On June 26, a Confederate column commanded by Stonewall Jackson himself began their march from Ashland toward the Richmond area. The column consisted of a line of skirmishers, about two hundred fifty feet in advance, followed by Reilly's Battery, prepared for instant action, then General Hood's brigade, and finally General Jackson. In the late afternoon, Jackson ordered Reilly's Battery to fire on a Federal cavalry unit trying to obstruct the road near a burnt bridge on the Jones farm. After firing twenty rounds, the battery routed the enemy, but General Jackson nevertheless ordered that they elevate their guns and fire another sixty rounds to encourage the Union horsemen to hasten their retreat.

Several times during the war, Captain Reilly displayed his mischievous sense of humor, and an incident on this march was one of those times. As the Texas Brigade under General Hood marched down the road, a Virginia farmer sat on the top rail of a fence singing the praises of the Confederacy. Unknown to the farmer intently watching the column in front of him, Captain Reilly was wheeling his battery into position behind him. The opening salvo with its great bang, billowing smoke and whistling projectiles that cleared his head by only a few feet, startled the farmer so that he fell backwards off the fence, scared to death. He jumped to his feet, took off running, cursing the Confederacy, and soon caught up with the Negroes who were working the fields. "Old Tarantula" was always full of tricks of this type and often demonstrated his sense of humor.

On June 27 the battery rejoined the Army of Northern Virginia and moved forward at sunrise to Gaines' Mill near the Chickahominy River to battle the Federal forces located there. Reilly's Battery did not become engaged until near sundown. The Confederate infantry had been hurled back again and again by a Federal battery equipped with three coffee mill guns and one three-inch ordnance rifle and located on the north side of the river. Captain Reilly's battery was ordered forward on the gallop, taking a position about three hundred yards from the Federal lines. They poured a devastating fire into the Yankees, and in twelve minutes the enemy's guns were silenced. At this close range, the force and accuracy of Reilly's rifled guns were awesome and very destructive. When the order to cease firing was given, General Hood's infantry rushed forward with a loud rebel yell and charged over the Yankees' breastworks to end the Battle of Gaines Mill.

The battery had expended one hundred rounds of ammunition. The three Union coffee mill guns (machine guns) remained where their gunners were killed or driven off. One of the Yankees' three-inch rifled guns had gotten stuck on a stump and had been abandoned. Colonel Evander M. Law and his men presented this beautiful gun to Captain Reilly's battery as a gift for their splendid service. Colonel Law, who came from Darlington, South Carolina and graduated from South Carolina Military Academy in 1856, later rose to the rank of general.

Reilly turned in one of the battery's Bellona rifled guns and replaced it with the Federal Parrott rifle. On the battlefield at Gaines' Mill Lieutenant John Ramsey found a bullet proof-type vest on a Yankee soldier and sent it home to Salisbury, North Carolina as a souvenir. Markings on the vest showed that it was made by the G and D Company of New Haven, Connecticut.

After their defeat at Gaines' Mill, the Federals pulled back across the Chickahominy River and moved into White Oak Swamp. Continuing his offensive, General Lee planned to drive the Federals from the swamp into the arms of General James Longstreet, whose corps was waiting on the other side. Another South Carolinian, Longstreet was born in Edgefield District, graduated West

Point in the Class of 1842, and served in the Indian and Mexican Wars. To make Lee's plan work and capture the entire Federal army, Stonewall Jackson had to move quickly to spring the trap. On June 30, Jackson's command, including Reilly's Battery, marched seven miles into White Oak Swamp and engaged the enemy's artillery and sharpshooters. After Reilly's Battery expelled four hundred and fifty rounds of ammunition, Jackson's Confederates drove the Federals into the swamp. However, Jackson uncharacteristically failed to pursue the enemy aggressively, allowing them several hours to escape through the swamp and engage General Longstreet to a stalemate at the Battle of Fraser's Farm. The Union army then withdrew to the amphitheatrical position of Malvern Hill.

Famous Confederate artillery commander General E. Porter Alexander, writing after the war, placed the blame for the Union escape squarely on Jackson, stating:

> *And now I shall have to tell as my narrative proceeds, of how upon several occasions in the progress of fighting during the next six days, General Lee's best hopes and plans were upset and miscarried, and how he was prevented from completely destroying and capturing McClellan's whole army and all its stores and artillery by the incredible slackness and delay and hanging back which characterized General Jackson's performance of his part of the work.*

Malvern Hill presented a superb artillery position, selected by General McClellan and his chief of artillery, General Henry J. Hunt. Rising sharply one hundred and fifty feet above an elevated plateau and flanked by two branches of the Western Run, streams and swamps, it created an excellent defensive position, allowing the Federal artillery to hold off the Confederates while General McClellan evacuated his army via Harrison's Landing on the James River under the protection of the Union gunboats.

Lieutenant Ramsay's eyewitness accounts of the Battle of Malvern Hill and Reilly's Battery's part in it speak for themselves.

> *July 1st the battery march[ed] four miles. In front of Malvern Hill Gen Whiting ordered Capt. Reilly and Lieutenant Ramsay to make a thorough reconnaissance of Malvern Hill and report to him. They had an excellent field glass, and rode over the field at a distance of about one hundred yards from the enemy's batteries. They reported that the enemy had thirty guns, in good position on ground higher than the opposite side of the valley, and that six of the guns were, in their opinion, twenty-pound Parrotts, and all*

of the others were either rifles or Napoleons. General Whiting said: "From the examination made, what plan of attack would you suggest?" Captain Reilly replied: "Our guns excepting those we have captured from the enemy, are inferior the theirs; many of our batteries have only four guns, while all of theirs have six, and I sug[g]est that we place eight in position at the same time. The distance is about one thousand yards, and smooth-bore guns are effective at that distance; the only trouble is that the range is not accurate." General Whiting designated the eight batteries that were to be sent forward, and sent his couriers to bring them up at once. The batteries were nearly ready to advance, when General Jackson rode up and asked why this delay. General Whiting explained the plan of attack. General Jackson replied that one battery was sufficient, and ordered Captain Reilly to advance at once, take a good position and commence the action. The battery took the best position it could get, and open[ed] fire on the enemy. The fire of the enemy's five battery's was concentrated on our one, and was terrific. The battery had been in action fifteen or twenty minutes, when General Whiting rode into the battery, and seeing the situation said: "Reilly, take your men out of this." Captain Reilly ordered the men to march by the right flank, and left the position. Expended one hundred and twenty-one rounds of ammunition. Twelve men were wounded: Milas Rufty, Robert Lentz, Abram Earnhardt, John Carter, Jonathan Hardister, Andrew Ruth, W. H. Huff, Ignaz Schoesser and Milas Parks. The Battery lost eight horses, including Lieutenant Ramsay's. After night the battery moved back one mile from the lines and encamped on Nelson's Farm.

According to a quotation found in the Lawrence Lee Papers, General D. H. Hill offered further perspective about the Battle of Malvern Hill, reporting that he saw General Jackson "helping with his own hands to push Reilly's North Carolina battery farther forward." For emphasis Hill added, "I noticed an artilleryman seated comfortably behind a large tree, and apparently feeling secure. A moment later a shell passed through the huge tree and took off the man's head. This gives an idea of the great power of the Federal rifled artillery."

Another account confirmed the savagery of the battle, stating "There was havoc with the battery — bones were not broken, they were severed, flesh was not pierced, it was shredded, blood did not trickle, it left the victims in torrents." Hill further observed that "it was not war, it was murder."

After ordering several bloody attacks at Malvern Hill, General Lee realized that the Federals would escape from Harrison's Landing via the James River and down the peninsula to Yorktown. The Confederate army and its men were too exhausted and disorganized to launch a pursuit, but Lee had saved Richmond from being captured. By saving the capital from the invading "Yankee horde," General

Lee gained the respect and admiration of both the army and the people of the South, a feeling that would only grow stronger as the war continued.

The Seven Days Battles, and especially Malvern Hill, revealed several disputes between the characters who made up the history of the Rowan Artillery. After the Seven Days, General Whiting was transferred to Wilmington, North Carolina. He did not like the way he was treated by Lee and Jackson, and complained bitterly about his "unnecessary" march up the valley to meet Jackson, only to turn around and march back to Richmond. While Lee planned this march to fool McClellan into thinking Jackson was being reinforced in preparation for an attack on Washington, D.C., Whiting felt it was unnecessary and did little to draw Union troops away from Richmond. Although the merits of his opinions are debatable, Whiting's sarcastic tone, his inflated ego, and his fondness for the bottle hurt his cause.

The final straw had been Jackson's interference with Whiting's artillery placements at Malvern Hill, which almost resulted in the destruction of Reilly's Battery. To understand the extent to which these events infuriated Whiting, we must also examine the two generals' shared history, going back to their days as West Point classmates. During this period Whiting ranked as the most academically brilliant cadet ever to attend the academy. He had felt sorry for Jackson, who was determined to graduate, but needed much tutoring. Whiting generously gave Jackson so much help that Jackson became known as "Whiting's Plebe." Neither man could realize that twenty years later Whiting would serve under Jackson's command. One can almost feel Whiting's animosity and anger over the hand that fate had dealt him.

Whiting was short, but had an aristocratic and noble appearance, with a slim figure, a well manicured mustache, dark eyes and graying hair. He had an impressive military bearing and courtly southern manners, the embodiment of a gallant cavalier from Mississippi. Extremely well read, Whiting's specialties were science and engineering. He drilled his troops with great vigor and was very attentive to their health and needs. This earned him the admiration and affection of his troops, who fondly nicknamed him "Little Billy."

Despite his excellent relationship with his troops, Whiting irritated and infuriated most of his superiors with his overconfidence and outright insubordination. He often expressed his sarcastic disdain for orders and ideas he thought foolish. This behavior was only tolerated because of Whiting's great talents and superior military skills, but "Little Billy" made a grave error when he offended President Jefferson Davis early in the war.

When General Joseph Johnston commanded Confederate forces in Virginia, President Davis ordered him to reorganize his army into brigades by their states of origin. Davis thought this would create a strong rivalry among the brigades. Critics believed that Davis designed this plan to enable troops from his home state of Mississippi to distinguish themselves from those of other Confederate states. General Whiting strongly opposed Davis's plan and, when selected to command one of the new Mississippi brigades, issued a typically blunt report. He informed the Confederate War Department that the president's plan was "a policy as suicidal as foolish….an inconceivable folly…solely for the advancement of log-rolling, humbugging politicians," and concluded with a direct statement, "I will not do it." This eventually led to Whiting's transfer to command of the District of Cape Fear, North Carolina, far from President Davis and the Army of Northern Virginia. At Wilmington, Whiting helped in the construction of Fort Fisher with over one thousand soldiers, workers and slaves, as well as two steam engines, at his disposal.

Historians still debate the reasons for Jackson's poor performance at the Seven Days. By the time of the Peninsula Campaign, Stonewall Jackson had already developed a reputation as a fierce fighter. The following quote perhaps best describes Jackson's image among most of the southern people. It appears in Mary Boykin Chesnut's book, *A Diary from Dixie*:

> *Don't you see this Stonewall, how he fires the soldiers? He will be our leader, maybe, after all. They say he does not care how many are killed. His business is to save the country, and not the army. If he can win, God bless him! And he wins. If they do not want to win, they can stay at home. They say he leaves sick and wounded to be cared for by those whose business it is to do so. His business is war. They say he will hoist the black flag, have a short, sharp, decisive war and end it! He is a Christian soldier. Let us drop all talk of the merciful Christ. They say Stonewall comes down on them like a house afire.*

When Stonewall Jackson started his march from the Shenandoah Valley to join the defenders of Richmond, he was without two key officers who had greatly contributed to his reputation, his success, and the swift movement of his army in the valley. The first was Captain James Keith Boswell, Jackson's engineer, who was invaluable in compiling and supplying his commander with information on roads and bridges, their type, construction and capacity for troops and artillery. The second key officer was Major Jedediah Hotchkiss, Jackson's famous mapmaker. Maps in many parts of the southern states were almost nonexistent. The few that were available were often poor in quality and gave little information as to the types and condition of roads and bridges and the distances between towns, villages, and other landmarks. Thus the team of Captain Boswell and Major Hotchkiss provided Stonewall Jackson with a tremendous technological advantage over his enemy in the valley.

At the Seven Days, however, Jackson was totally in the dark, with no skilled mapmaker or engineer. The entire Confederate command, including General Lee, struggled with insufficient maps, and this deficiency made Jackson unsure of himself and uncharacteristically slow in his movements.

It was also a well known fact that Jackson required an abundant amount of sleep and could fall asleep at any time or in any place. Several accounts document the devout Christian general falling asleep in church. By the time he neared Richmond, he was extremely tired. This physical exhaustion, coupled with the absence of proper geographic guides, likely caused his poor judgment and performance during the Seven Days Battles.

One can easily understand how much anger the officers and men of Reilly's Battery must have felt toward Stonewall Jackson, since his orders resulted in numerous casualties. If General Whiting had not come to their aid and ordered them to withdraw, the entire battery might have been lost. These events had far reaching future effects on Captain Reilly.

The artillery tactics used at Malvern Hill by Union General H. J. Hunt, Reilly's friend from earlier days in Federal service, were crucial to saving the Federal army. Hunt's tactics remained the same throughout the war. He liked to mass a large number of guns to fire on one enemy position. He often massed four Federal batteries, or a battalion of approximately twenty-four guns, to fire on a Confederate battery of only four to six guns. After that position was expelled or destroyed, he concentrated his fire on the next chosen target. Hunt advocated conserving artillery rounds by firing at a slower rate, aiming the guns precisely to inflict maximum damage and destruction to the enemy.

At Malvern Hill, Hunt commanded over three hundred and forty guns of all sizes and calibers, including large siege guns. He positioned his artillery in tiers on the crests of the hills, covering the ground in front of the Confederates and protecting the Union retreat. His field of fire was so powerful that any type of Confederate artillery or infantry attack would have been suicidal, a fact which General Lee soon realized. Personally directing one group of sixty guns, Hunt employed them as though they were a single battery. His superior artillery position and tactics gave the Union army valuable time to escape from the Army of

Northern Virginia. From a perspective of over a century later, it is interesting to speculate whether General Hunt recognized his enemy as his old, tough, Irish drill sergeant, and to wonder whether Captain Reilly realized that Hunt would employ his famous mass artillery firing tactics against Reilly's Battery.

CHAPTER III

THE SECOND MANASSAS CAMPAIGN

Following the Battle of Malvern Hill, the Rowan Artillery moved to Nelson's Farm, about one mile from the battle line. On July 9, the battery redeployed to Meadow Bridge Road, roughly one and a half miles from Richmond. Here, they rested, repaired their guns, and resupplied their ammunition and equipment. Artillery drills resumed on July 21.

At the same time, the battery sent nineteen condemned horses to Richmond to be replaced. To the men's delight, they received forty-five excellent artillery horses as replacements. One of these strong and active horses replaced Lieutenant Ramsay's mount, which had been shot out from under him at Malvern Hill. On August 7, the battery began its march north. Captain Reilly who had remained behind, rejoined the battery on August 10 with twenty new recruits, obtained while in Richmond. Now the battery had regained full strength and excellent fighting condition.

The battery continued its march northward to Hanover Junction, reaching Orange Court House on August 17. At Kelly's Ford on the Hazel River on August 22 and 23, the battery engaged the enemy for the first time since Malvern Hill, firing forty rounds of ammunition. An incident that took place at this time reveals more of Captain Reilly's Irish sense of humor. Recounted by Colonel Harold B. Simpson in *Hood's Texas Brigade: Lee's Grenadier Guard* with Reilly's brogue, it goes as follows:

> *Here it was that Captain Reilly, commanding one of the batteries attached to the brigade, let his imperfection of sight lead him into trouble with his superiors. While yet the cannonading on both sides was in progress, a lone horseman rode into the river at the ford, bearing a white flag. Swearing that although he could see the man and horse distinctly, he could see no flag, Reilly trained and fired a gun at the fellow, the round shot plunging into*

the water three feet to his right. That not calling him to a halt, Captain Reilly, still insisting that he could see no white flag, fired two more shots, one which struck the water a few feet to the left of the horseman and the other, five feet in front of him. Hardly, though, was the last shot on its way, when an aide de camp dispatched by General Hood came at full speed and halted near Captain Reilly, shouting: "General Hood says stop your damned foolishness — that man is bearing a flag of truce."

"An' so, be Jasus, he is," confessed Reilly with a grin, "but in the name of St. Pathrick an' all the ither hoully saints, whoy didn't the spalpeen hould the dommed white rag high enough for an Irishman to persaive it?"

As the rider came near the Confederate lines, it became apparent that he was a staff officer and the flag he carried was in fact a signal flag rather than a flag of truce. The officer and his horse were unhurt. He had crossed the lines to ask for a ceasefire to bury the dead.

A new reorganization of the Army of Northern Virginia attached the Rowan Artillery to the Texas Division, commanded by Whiting's former subordinate, John Bell Hood, in General James Longstreet's First Corps. Thus Reilly and his battery came under the command of Longstreet's Chief of Artillery, Colonel James B. Walton. Born in Newark, New Jersey, but raised in New Orleans, Walton attended Louisiana College and served in the Mexican War. He began his Confederate service as commander of the famous Washington Artillery of New Orleans. This somewhat large man made an imposing and gallant figure in his Confederate uniform astride his large coal-black stallion named "Rebel."

The new battalion commander, thirty-six year old Virginian Major Bushrod Washington Frobel, had worked as a civil engineer in the United States Revenue Service before the war. Even though he had considerable artillery experience, Frobel found himself assigned to General Whiting's staff during the Seven Days Battles. Records show that Frobel, a native of Alexandria, applied for admission to West Point, but never attended. He graduated from the Episcopal High School and Theological Seminary of Virginia, where William Nelson Pendleton served as principal, giving him a strong personal connection to the highest ranking officer in the artillery of the Army of Northern Virginia.

Part of General Lee's reorganization involved the transfer of General Whiting to the Department of North Carolina. Whiting reported to Wilmington, where he was put in charge of organizing and building defenses along the Cape Fear River. At Wilmington, Whiting used his engineering genius and skills to help construct the famous Fort Fisher with over one thousand soldiers, workers, and slaves at his disposal, as well as two steam engines. Eventually, he and his old friend, Captain Reilly, would reunite to defend Fort Fisher and Wilmington from the Federal army and the Union fleet.

Reilly's Battery continued its march northward with Generals Longstreet and Lee to support Stonewall Jackson's movement against the new Federal army commanded by General John Pope at Manassas, Virginia, site of the previous year's Confederate victory. General Pope was born in Louisville, Kentucky, and graduated from the United States Military Academy in the Class of 1842. A veteran of the Mexican War, he had performed admirably against the Confederates in the western theater, primarily along the Mississippi River.

Abraham Lincoln had removed General George McClellan from command of the Army of the Potomac for his poor performance during the Peninsula Campaign. General Pope's command, designated the Army of Virginia, consisted of large portions of the Army of the Potomac, as well as other Union forces gathered from throughout Virginia. Soon after taking command, Pope made a rather rash and condescending statement to his men, declaring that "I come from the West where we have seen the backs of our enemies." This did not sit well with his army and did not help him in his efforts to win a campaign against the emotionally committed Army of Northern Virginia under General Lee, or as his men now affectionately called him, "Marse Robert."

On August 26, 1862, the Rowan Artillery encamped near Sperryville, Virginia, along with the other batteries in their battalion. These included the South Carolina German Artillery with Captain W. K. Bachman in command and the South Carolina Palmetto Artillery, commanded by Captain Hugh R. Garden.

By August 28, Reilly's Battery led the Confederate column, pushing through Manassas and Thoroughfare Gaps near Manassas, Virginia. Where a little creek ran through one particular gap, a railroad had been built along the north side and a very narrow turnpike along the south side. While the Confederate force waited to move forward, the Union artillery at the opposite end of the gap opened fire, sending what Ramsay described as "a maelstrom of shot and shell through the gap at us that halted our column." At five in the afternoon Reilly received an order to bring the battery's four rifled guns forward. Since these guns occupied the rear of the column, the infantry had to move to one side in the narrow gap to make room for Lieutenant Ramsay to bring the guns forward at a rapid gallop. As Ramsay neared the gap, Colonel Walton and a second man galloped alongside him. Walton said, "Here is your guide. He will show you a fine position, and give them Hell."

After advancing one hundred and fifty yards through the gap with the guide, the battery now faced a storm of shot and shell. The guide said, "There is some mistake here, and I must go and see Colonel Walton." He turned his horse and started back. Lieutenant Ramsay ordered the battery to halt and hold their position. After waiting twenty minutes, Ramsay sent Bugler Peeler to find Colonel Walton and report that the guide had left. Unable to sight their guns accurately, Ramsay and his gunners awaited further instructions. After Peeler had been gone twenty minutes or longer, Ramsay, realizing that both the guide and Peeler might have been killed, sent Guidon Hall, the flag bearer, back to find Colonel Walton.

A few minutes later, Major Sellers, General Hood's adjutant, came up the railroad tracks on foot and said, "Ramsay, what are you doing here?" Lieutenant Ramsay replied, "Colonel Walton ordered us in here to find a good position." Major Sellers replied, "I have been up close to the enemy's lines and there is no position anywhere in the gap than this." Ramsay turned to his men and said, "We have got to get our battery out of this. Climb this mountain!" He placed great emphasis on the last three words.

Now safe, and for the time being out of harm's way, the Rowan Artillery camped on the plains of Manassas. But this feeling of security would not even last a full day. On August 29, the day following the Battle of Thoroughfare Gap, the battery marched nine miles to take a position on the right side of the Warrenton Turnpike. There they engaged the Federals with four rifled guns. This came as quite a surprise to the Yankee infantry, who were already under heavy fire from Stonewall Jackson's troops. The battery's placement at an angle to the Yankee lines created a perfect position to enfilade their formation. Pouring fifty-five rounds into the Union troops caused great destruction and confusion.

This bombardment forced the enemy to change its front lines and establish a new line of battle. Not to be outmaneuvered, Reilly's men moved their four guns to an excellent position on a ridge at right angles to, and about three hundred yards to the left of, the Warrenton Turnpike. The Washington Artillery occupied the position between Reilly's guns and the turnpike. A fierce artillery duel began. The guns of the Rowan Artillery grew so hot that the gunners could not touch them.

The left gun of the right section fired a round without a friction primer, because the heat of the gun barrel itself ignited the charge. This very dangerous situation created a high probability for a misfire, as the crew rammed the round into the breach. The men solved this problem by raising the tube and emptying their canteens down the muzzle. The water cooled the gun tube down most effectively, allowing the gun to return to action safely. An overheated gun could also cause the tube to burst, sending metal flying in all directions, killing bystanders as well as members of the gun crew. Guns made during this era often overheated and burst.

As the battle continued, Reilly's Battery exhausted their ammunition. Finding their limber chests empty, the men temporarily withdrew to procure a fresh supply of rounds. By the time they returned, the enemy had retreated. In this action the battery expended six hundred and fifty rounds of ammunition, an unusually large volume of projectiles. With such a high rate of fire, Reilly's Battery was fortunate not to suffer a burst tube or a misfire. Five of the battery's horses were killed during the action, four by one solid shot from a Union gun, an indication of the powerful velocity of projectiles during the War Between the States.

On the afternoon of August 30, the entire battery was placed on the right side of the turnpike, where they again engaged the enemy. The Rowan Artillery kept up a destructive and steady fire, this time expending five hundred and twenty rounds of ammunition. Unfortunately, during this action, Lieutenant Ramsay was slightly wounded when the base, or sabo, of a large twenty-pound Parrott shell struck him on the right knee. Fortunately, the shell was spent and struck at a very low velocity, causing him only some bruising. He was again very lucky.

General Lee was also injured on the last day at Second Manassas. While dismounted near a railroad embankment, he held his horse's bridle when the animal suddenly threw his head up and jumped backwards. Lee was thrown violently to the ground, spraining both of his wrists and breaking a small bone in one hand. As a result, he could not ride and had to use his ambulance wagon for transportation, a circumstance which impacted the history of the Rowan Artillery in the subsequent campaign.

The Federal Army of Virginia, commanded by General John Pope, retreated from Manassas on August 31, 1862. Reilly's Battery camped near the famous "Stone House," the Henry P. Matthews house on the Manassas battlefield.

The famed Union artillery commander, General Henry J. Hunt, did not participate in the Battle of Second Manassas. He was at Aquia Creek, trying to untangle batteries and reorganize confused artillerymen after the Peninsula Campaign, and did not receive sufficient notice to support General Pope. The Federal batteries at Second Manassas were commanded by officers handpicked by Pope, and did not affect a mass firing as Hunt had at Malvern Hill. According to Confederate artillerists, the Union guns "frittered away their efforts as individuals."

Among his other contributions, General Hunt instituted a program of uniformity in the caliber and type of cannon within each six-gun battery. Under this program, each Union battery contained the same type of guns. The Federal army had strictly Parrott rifle batteries and strictly Napoleon gun batteries, but never mixed guns within a battery as the Confederate artillery did. This gave the Federals a tremendous advantage, making it much easier to reload limber chests and caissons at the ammunition supply train.

Hunt also created an effective artillery reserve of one hundred guns. This reserve helped replace and reinforce frontline Union guns when needed. As Hunt explained:

> *In marches near the enemy it is often desirable to occupy positions with guns for special purposes: to command fords, to cover the throwing and taking up of bridges, and for many other purposes for which it would be inconvenient and inadvisable to withdraw their batteries from the troops. Hence the necessity for a reserve of artillery.*

During each campaign, Hunt insisted on having his famous siege train accompany the Union artillery. The siege train was made up of large guns, consisting of four and a half inch ordnance rifles, eight-inch Howitzers and thirty-pound Parrott rifles. Moving these very large guns in the field slowed troop movements and required vast numbers of horses, mules and oxen to pull the heavy and cumbersome loads. Despite these drawbacks, Hunt believed the train was indispensable when operating in Confederate territory.

With General Lee's victory at Second Manassas, the defeated Federal army streamed back to the protection of the fortifications surrounding Washington, D.C. President Lincoln reluctantly restored "Little Mac" McClellan to reorganize and command the Army of the Potomac. The Union troops affectionately welcomed McClellan back.

While the northern armies seemed powerless to defeat Robert E. Lee's Army of Northern Virginia, the "Anaconda Plan" formulated by General Winfield Scott at the outset of the war slowly had its effect on the Confederacy. With southern ports blockaded, it became increasingly difficult to get much needed military supplies to the Confederate armies and vital materials to the southern people.

The Confederate government had sent ambassadors to England and France to seek those nations' assistance with supplies and possible military intervention in the war. The British prime minister, Lord Palmerston, said he could not support the slave-holding South, although England would love to see the United States divided into two nations. Slavery provided a convenient excuse for a British government suspicious that the French, the Germans, or the Russians might attack them, should they send troops to aid the Confederacy.

The Confederate government was under the firm belief and impression that England would be bound to help support the Confederate cause with British troops and industrial military goods because England needed an uninterrupted supply of southern cotton to help keep the economically important Manchester cotton mills running. However, the Confederacy was surprised that England was able to procure all its cotton needs from India, cutting out its demand for Confederate cotton. This move by England was quite an unexpected blow to the Confederate government and its war effort.

While the upper classes of England favored the Confederacy, the lower classes generally supported the Union. However, the British government was much more concerned about being "stabbed in the back" in Europe, particularly by the cunning and conspiratorial Emperor Napoleon III of France, than it was in supporting either side in the American conflict.

CHAPTER IV

SOUTH MOUNTAIN TO FREDERICKSBURG

Having inflicted a crushing defeat on Pope's army at Manassas, General Lee, with the approval of President Davis, decided to strike a blow against the Union on its own ground. Thus began the Confederate army's invasion of Maryland. The entire countryside around the battlefields of Virginia was depleted of food and fodder. The army also desperately needed new recruits, which they believed would be plentiful in Maryland. By September 1, Reilly's Battery was on the march with Longstreet's Corps, Hood's Division, and Major B. W. Frobel's Artillery. Frobel's Artillery consisted of two hundred ninety-six men and sixteen guns and included Captain W. K. Bachman's "German" Charleston Artillery with six guns, Captain Garden's "Palmetto" South Carolina Battery with four guns and Captain Reilly's Rowan North Carolina Battery with six guns. The men of the Confederate army were in high spirits and sang such popular songs as Maryland, My Maryland, Dixie, The Bonnie Blue Flag, and The Girl I Left Behind Me, as they marched along while the military bands played.

On September 7, Frobel's Artillery crossed the Potomac River and encamped near Bucktown, Maryland. By the twelfth, having passed through Frederick Junction and Middleton, Maryland, they marched to within two miles of Hagerstown, where they halted to procure supplies. The men and horses had been without rations for twenty-four hours. In this part of Maryland, the inhabitants proved to be loyal to the Union and refused to sell supplies or firewood to the Confederates. Finally some firewood was procured and the rations were cooked on the fire.

About one o'clock in the afternoon a courier galloped up with orders to proceed as quickly as possible to South Mountain and report to General Daniel Harvey Hill. The bugler blew assembly, and the horses, having already been fed, were quickly harnessed. The drivers and cannoneers took some of the half cooked rations from the fire and within seven minutes the battery was again rumbling over the National Road.

The emergency, which required the artillerymen to abandon their long awaited meal, resulted from a surprising series of events. General Lee's Special Orders Number 191, which outlined his disposition of the Army of Northern Virginia for its advance into Maryland, were inadvertently dropped by a courier. Corporal Barton Mitchell, of the Twenty-Seventh Indiana Infantry, found these orders wrapped around a few cigars in an abandoned Confederate camp outside Frederick, Maryland on September 13, 1862.

This crucial find was immediately rushed to General McClellan's headquarters. McClellan in turn telegraphed President Lincoln, informing him, "I have all the plans of the rebels." With the "lost orders" in his hands, "Little Mac" uncharacteristically moved with great speed to push Lee's troops through the gaps at South Mountain and back to Sharpsburg. There, McClellan hoped to trap Lee with his back to the Potomac River and crush the Army of Northern Virginia.

The Rowan Artillery's division commander, General John Bell Hood, who had led a powerful attack at the Battle of Second Manassas, was now under arrest by order of General Nathan G. Evans over a dispute about captured wagons and ambulances. Nevertheless, General Hood was allowed to accompany his division, and was officially released by General Lee on the morning of McClellan's attack at South Mountain. Lee realized that this was no time for petty ego disputes between his generals.

For the Union leadership, the results of this campaign were crucial, politically as well as militarily. Throughout the summer, President Lincoln and his cabinet had faced a dilemma over how to keep the European powers from coming to the aid of the Confederacy and at the same time satisfy the ever-mounting pressure from abolitionists in the North. Lincoln proposed a preliminary Emancipation Proclamation as a way to address both situations. The European powers would not openly back a "slave holding" nation against an "anti-slavery" one, and the abolitionists would rejoice that action was finally being taken to free southern slaves.

Lincoln came to this position reluctantly. A believer in segregation, who had initially favored returning the slaves to Africa or establishing a segregated state for them in America, he had long insisted that he was waging the war to save the Union, not to free the slaves. At this point his proposed proclamation only intended to free slaves within the Confederacy and not the hundreds of Blacks held in slavery in northern states and the new territories.

By July 1862, Lincoln read his preliminary Emancipation Proclamation to his cabinet, but decided to wait for a Union military victory to issue it, feeling that on the heels of the Union defeat in the Seven Days, it would appear to be an act of desperation. The additional defeat at Second Manassas and the increasingly unstable international situation made the upcoming campaign extremely important for the politically conniving "damn Yankees." As it turned out, the Emancipation Proclamation proved to be an excellent political strategy.

The Rowan Artillery arrived at Turner Gap at South Mountain about three o'clock in the afternoon on September 14 and took the position assigned directly by General Hill. The right section was anchored near Hill's headquarters, a one hundred and thirty-year-old stone hotel named South Mountain Inn. In 1876 Madeline Vinton Dahlgren, the wealthy widow of the famous Union admiral, John A. Dahlgren, purchased the inn. Dahlgren, a famed artillerist, invented the well-known Dahlgren cannons, which mainly saw action as very large and powerful naval guns aboard Union warships. Union marines used the smaller Dahlgren boat howitzers to assist them in amphibious landings. The hotel is still in use today and houses a famous historical gourmet restaurant, Old South Mountain Inn.

As he positioned Reilly's Battery, General Hill issued special orders, "Do not fire unless ordered to do so, or our troops are pushed up the mountain and past the battery." The battery came under enemy fire for the rest of the day, but under these orders Old Tarantula could not respond in kind. His Irish temper and impatience with the enemy must have made the situation virtually unbearable for him. Not until about an hour after sunset did the battery redeploy and camp near the foot of South Mountain out of range of the Federal artillery.

On September 15, 1862, the Rowan Artillery was ordered to protect the Army of Northern Virginia as part of its rear guard. They marched eight miles, where they took their position on the right side of a road leading from Sharpsburg to the stone bridge across Antietam Creek. Mid-morning, General Hood, mounted on his horse, "Thunder," ordered Lieutenant Ramsay to position one of his three-inch rifled guns on a little ridge three hundred yards to the left of the road and three hundred fifty yards in front of the battle line. Ramsay was to fire into the woods to his front, and retire if the Federals made his position "hot."

After the rifled gun fired about twelve shots, the Yankees returned fire, making it so hot that the other rifled batteries positioned along the heights opened on the enemy to relieve Ramsay. After firing twenty-one rounds of ammunition, Ramsay's piece withdrew to its former position with the rest of the battery without any loss of men or horses. General Hood rode up and offered his compliments to Lieutenant Ramsay and the gun crew for their brave and gallant execution of his orders. The rest of the day produced only picket firing. The battery encamped under their guns near the line of battle in preparation for what would become the bloodiest day in American military history, the Battle of Sharpsburg. The Yankees called it the Battle of Antietam Creek.

On Tuesday, September 16, the prelude to the main battle at Sharpsburg began. General McClellan had pushed the remainder of Lee's army through the gaps of South Mountain to a point near Antietam Creek, where he hoped to trap and destroy the Confederates. General Lee faced the overwhelming task of re-concentrating his army to hold back the impending disaster and escape back across the Potomac River to the safety of Virginia.

The Rowan Artillery joined the action at ten o'clock in the morning. Two sections of rifled guns, composed of two three-inch rifles commanded by Lieutenant J. F. Woodard and two ten-pound Parrott rifles commanded by Lieutenant Ramsay, received orders to engage the enemy and maintain a steady well-directed fire until ordered to redeploy. After expending four hundred and eighty-four rounds of ammunition and with two horses killed and one wounded and abandoned, the battery was ordered to retire to the rear, refill their ammunition chest and encamp.

On Wednesday, September 17, the actual Battle of Sharpsburg began. Reilly's Battery was now scrambled and placed in different parts of the battlefield in order to take best advantage of their diverse firing range and types of projectiles. The left section, commanded by Lieutenant William W. Myers, consisted of two twenty-four pound howitzers, excellent cannons for use against infantry at close range. The center section consisted of two three-inch rifled guns, commanded by Lieutenant J. H. Woodard, and the right section contained two ten-pound Parrott rifles commanded by Lieutenant Ramsay.

Early in the morning, the battery's two rifled sections proceeded with the rest of Major Frobel's Battalion to oppose the Union advance from the cornfield and around the Dunkard Church. Reilly's Battery fired into the enemy with devastating effect until their ammunition was exhausted and they retreated to the rear to refill their ammunition chest.

An interesting incident which occurred on this day may have involved Reilly's Battery. A group of Federal officers, riding near and surveying the Confederate lines, came in full view and perfect range of a Confederate battery. "Let's give them a shot," cried one cannoneer, but another gunner said, "No, that's the chief of artillery [General Hunt]. He rides that white horse and is a brave man and I won't fire on him. We will wait until the battery comes and we will fire at that." It would have been a terrible trick of fate for the Union army, if the Confederates had fired and killed General Hunt, Reilly's friend and former commander.

Meanwhile, the howitzer section of the battery under Lieutenant Myers engaged the enemy at the lower stone bridge crossing Antietam Creek, now known as Burnside's Bridge. Union General Ambrose Burnside attempted to cross the lower bridge and attack Lee's flank. The Confederates held Burnside's advance until about noon before being overwhelmed. Federal infantry and artillery then poured over the bridge, pushing the rebels back. During this assault, the howitzer section of the Rowan Artillery suffered greatly from Hunt's massed artillery fire. All their horses were killed and they had to draw their guns back to safety by hand to avoid capture. One gun was totally disabled; three men were killed, two wounded and two missing.

For reasons still unknown to students of the battle, Burnside halted his advance and stopped to eat lunch and reorganize his troops. This proved to be a godsend for the Army of Northern Virginia and General Lee, giving them time to strengthen their defensive position and pray for reinforcements to arrive and save them from certain destruction. Once again, the Union artillery was commanded by the old artillery master, General Henry J. Hunt. Fate, again, placed Reilly and Hunt opposite each other on the field, where Hunt employed his mass firing strategy against Confederate artillery. More than five hundred cannons participated in the battle, firing over fifty thousand rounds of ammunition. The cannonading was so intense that Confederate artillery commander, Colonel S.D. Lee, called it "artillery hell."

Whoever had the most guns during the many battles of the War Between the States would likely emerge victorious. The psychological effects and confusion were overwhelming. Extreme noise levels of the guns, exploding of case and shell overhead and the agonizing screams of men being wounded and killed were deafening. The sight of men in close proximity being blown apart, their blood and body liquids splattered over other troops, was horrifying. Intestines, bones, heads, and other body sections lay strung in the tops of trees and scattered over the battleground in a great river of gore. The odor of fresh flesh being torn from bodies and the putrid smell of flesh left to rot assaulted the senses. Horrible sights and sounds included horses being killed and wounded, struggling to escape without legs and eyes as large as saucers from fear and panic. These were just a few of the terrifying scenes the brave men on both sides had to overcome as they marched or charged straight into the enemy's artillery batteries. The devastation caused by artillery was hard for any man or beast to endure, comprehend or overcome.

After Burnside's delay at the lower stone bridge, he finally ordered his troops to push Lee's right flank. Without reinforcements, Lee now fully realized his army's extremely dangerous position. One can only imagine the devout Confederate commander silently reciting his favorite psalm, calling on the Lord to help him and the Army of Northern Virginia in these words, "Blessed be the Lord my rock! Who trains my hand to fight and my fingers to battle. My help and my fortress, my stronghold and my deliverer, my shield in whom I trust, who subdues the peoples under me."

About three in the afternoon the right section of ten-pound Parrott rifles, commanded by Lieutenant Ramsay, returned to the front after obtaining a fresh supply of ammunition. General Lee and several other officers tried to rally the men into line. Seeing that Lieutenant Ramsay had a telescope, Lee said to him, "What troops are those?," pointing to the position formerly held by Captain Reilly's battery. Ramsay drew his telescope from the case and handed it to General Lee. Lee held up his wounded hands, fingers still in bandages from his fall at the Battle of Second Manassas, and said, "I can't use it; what troops are those?" Ramsay dismounted and adjusted the glass, replying, "They are flying the United States flag." General Lee then pointed at another body of troops, nearly at right angles from the others, and asked, "What troops are those?" Lieutenant Ramsay responded, "They are flying the Virginia and Confederate flags." General Lee realized that it was A. P. Hill from Harper's Ferry. He ordered Ramsay to place his guns on a little knoll to the right of the road and fire on "those people," pointing in the first-named direction.

Lieutenant Ramsay remarked, "General Lee, as soon as we fire, we will draw the enemy's fire." Lee replied, "Never mind." The right section Rowan gunners, James M. Pitman and Ignaz Schoesser, expertly fired the first shell into the middle of the enemy line and the next a short distance to the right of the first. By the time each gun had thrown five shells, the enemy had disappeared. General Lee, smiling, said, "Well done! Elevate your guns and continue the fire," ordering Ramsay to direct his fire on successive waves of enemy troops and then to change his position to a ridge from which he could fire on the troops beyond the creek. General Lee then rode away on his famous gray horse, "Traveller."

The battery followed Lee's orders until darkness closed the action. The Rowan Artillery expended fifty-six rounds of ammunition at their first position and two hundred at their second without suffering any losses. The center section of three-inch rifles under Lieutenant Woodard could not get ammunition and was therefore not engaged.

General A. P. Hill's arrival from Harper's Ferry saved the Army of Northern Virginia in a nick of time. Hill smashed into Burnside's left flank, driving him back. This day, September 17, 1862, was the bloodiest single day in American history with a total of twenty-three thousand men killed or wounded. The Army of Northern Virginia now moved rapidly to extract itself from Sharpsburg and cross the Potomac River to the safety of Virginia.

The battle was a shallow victory for the Union, however. General McClellan had attacked piecemeal, causing each attack to fail. If he had made an all-out attack, he would have overwhelmed Lee with his superior force and crushed the Confederate Army. President Lincoln was extremely upset that "Little Mac" let Lee's army escape, but nevertheless used this "victory" to publicly issue the Emancipation Proclamation on September 22, 1862.

The day after the Battle of Sharpsburg the men of Reilly's Battery were commanded to "trot march," but did not obey. The men and horses were "give out," having been on the field of battle four days, the last two and a half without rations. The time they took to rest provides the backdrop for "Old Tarantula" and the rear guard action of Reilly's Battery.

Corps commander, General James Longstreet, ordered his chief of artillery, Colonel J. B. Walton, to provide one battery to cover the Confederate withdrawal from Sharpsburg. Colonel Walton dispatched Captain William M. Owen, a thirty-year-old staff officer from New Orleans and a member of the Washington Artillery, to select the battery. Captain Owen had to find a battery still in Sharpsburg. He had almost reached Shepherdstown, Virginia, tired and weary, when he turned his horse around and returned to Sharpsburg to complete his orders. A dense fog and blinding smoke from bonfires that soldiers had lit to mark the line of march to the Potomac River filled the road.

Soldiers on the road constantly streamed around Owen and his horse and when he nudged by one of them, they hurled insults and cursed him. Some even suggested that he was "going after buttermilk." Owen rode as far as he needed, then reined his horse to a halt and waited. He soon heard the clanking and jangling of a battery through the mist to the east. "Whose battery is that?," he shouted. "Captain Reilly's." "Ah, Captain! Just looking for you," Owen replied as the guns came into view. "The chief of artillery directs you to halt here and report to General Jeb Stuart as he comes by with his rear guard." "Devil take it now," Reilly growled with his thick Irish brogue. Captain Owen took a drink from his pocket whiskey flask. Reilly continued, "Can't somebody else do this? My men are tired out. Let me get beyond the river." "Couldn't think of it, Captain," Owen teased Old Tarantula. "This is the post of honor. Report to Stuart. Good-bye and good luck to you." As Captain Owen turned his horse around and vanished into the heavy fog, Captain Reilly verbally assaulted him from a distance with oaths, concluding, "Dang all posts of honor!"

General James Ewell Brown "Jeb" Stuart, born in Patrick County, Virginia in 1833, attended Emory and Henry College for two years before entering West Point, where he graduated thirtieth in the class of 1854. As Lee's chief of cavalry, Stuart was swashbuckling in appearance and style with his famous plumed hat and dashing uniform, as he rode his horse, "Highfly."

More than likely, as parts of Stuart's horse artillery under the command of Captain John Pelham passed Reilly's Battery to become part of the rear guard, the men of the battery did not realize that a brave young artillery officer from Kentucky in Pelham's unit would soon become their new battalion commander.

After a few minor artillery duels during the retreat, the Rowan Artillery finally crossed the Potomac. By September 20 they encamped near the Occoquan River, two miles from Martinsburg, Virginia. By the twenty-ninth, they set up camp on the Martinsburg Road, six miles from Winchester. During this march, a limber chest accidentally exploded, killing Private Lorenzo Bullaboa of Rowan County, North Carolina and Private John W. Draughorn of Sampson County, North Carolina.

On October 10, 1862, under special orders from headquarters, one sergeant, one corporal and forty-three men were transferred from Captain Whitnel Pugh Lloyd's battery (Third North Carolina Artillery, Company G) of Jackson's Corps to the Rowan Artillery. Captain Lloyd resided in Edgecombe County, the county seat being Tarboro, North Carolina. He resigned from the Army of Northern Virginia at age twenty-six because of poor health, including hernia problems. His men, guns and horses were disbanded and combined with other artillery batteries.

Thus reinforced, Reilly's Battery began a march on October 29 that would not culminate until December 3, when they reached Culpeper Court House, Virginia. During this time, General Lee ordered General W. N. Pendleton to provide him with an evaluation of battery commanders and their performances in the recent battles. Pendleton quickly narrowed the list of outstanding performances to fourteen batteries out of sixty. He ranked Captain Thomas H.

Carter from Pampatike, Virginia, a distant relative of General Lee, first in the Army of Northern Virginia's artillery. Captain Carter, later promoted to colonel, had graduated from Virginia Military Institute in 1849 and then the University of Virginia. He also completed the medical course at the University of Pennsylvania. He was widely considered a true Christian and a most noble Virginia gentleman. Pendleton rated Carter's battery, the King William Artillery, first for its outstanding ability in maneuvering in and out of battlefield positions with speed and correct procedure, for above average placement of its guns, for excellent marksmanship and drill, and for Carter's attention to details in the overall appearance of his battery.

Pendleton rated Captain Reilly's Battery second because of the very good condition of guns, horses, and men, especially noting the soft, pliable and buttery condition of the battery's leather tack. Reilly knew and employed a little-known procedure of boiling the hoofs of animals and reducing the substance down to make oil. Today this oil is known as neatsfoot oil, an excellent leather preservative and softener. Reilly's men and guns also appeared in very good condition, which added to the overall showing of the battery.

On November 7, the Rowan Artillery faced another evaluation when the inspector general of the Army of Northern Virginia, Colonel Edwin J. Harvie, inspected Major Frobel's Battalion. Harvie, too, expressed his excellent impression of the overall appearance and condition of Reilly's Battery.

Praise was plentiful, but it did not bring promotion for Captain Reilly, a fact which was beginning to play heavily on Reilly's mind. The captain's resentment would soon boil over, causing Reilly to seek assistance from Governor Zebulon Vance of North Carolina. An examination of the silent parameters the Army of Northern Virginia used for higher promotions in the officer corps sheds a bright light on Reilly's difficulties. A considerable number of the officers promoted to higher ranks of command represented the southern aristocracy, particularly from Virginia, and were politically well connected, wealthy, "high on the goose," and preferably educated at West Point or the Virginia Military Institute. Almost all could be described as native-born southern Protestant gentlemen. Unfortunately, Captain Reilly met none of these criteria, which conspired silently and unofficially to hold him back in rank. Reilly needed someone with strong political power and influence to intervene on his behalf.

By December 11, Reilly's Battery arrived at Fredericksburg, Virginia, where General Lee gathered his forces on the south side of the Rappahannock River to intercept the Army of the Potomac, as it again advanced on Richmond. General

Ambrose E. Burnside, whose corps Reilly's men had faced at Sharpsburg, now commanded the one hundred and twenty thousand man Army of the Potomac. President Lincoln had again removed General McClellan from command, this time because of his failure to destroy Lee after Sharpsburg. Even with overwhelming numbers, possession of Lee's battle plans and superior ground positions, he failed to crush the Army of Northern Virginia, because of his constant reluctance to take action.

General Burnside, an Indiana native and West Point graduate in the Class of 1847, was a successful and politically connected Rhode Island businessman when the war began. On assuming command of the army, Burnside developed a bold plan to capture Richmond and secured Lincoln's approval. He proposed crossing the Rappahannock River and surprising Lee with a direct, swift and decisive move against the Confederate capital. This plan only failed because Lee quickly and insightfully gathered his army at Fredericksburg, where he placed them in a very strategic position on the heights overlooking the town. Burnside was delayed several days, waiting for the arrival of the pontoon bridges necessary to cross the river. When the bridges finally arrived, Confederate sharpshooters held back the Federal engineers from placing them into position to allow the Union army to cross.

Once the Union army finally did cross the wide river, they had to move through the town, then across a wide expanse of open ground to attack an enemy heavily entrenched on the heights. This proved to be a military nightmare, which needlessly caused the deaths of thousands of Union soldiers. Like McClellan and Pope, Burnside was destined to taste the bitterness of defeat at the hands of General Lee and the Army of Northern Virginia.

From December 11 through December 16, 1862, the Rowan Artillery occupied a position on high ground near the Dr. Reynolds house, "Lansdowne," in front of the enemy. "Landsdowne" was a one-story wood frame white house with a porch across the front and dormer windows, built on a high terraced hill with lovely gardens of flowers and shrubs. At the time of the Battle of Fredericksburg, Dr. Reynolds was forty-eight years old, his wife Caroline was thirty-two, and they had three children. They owned and farmed eight hundred and thirty acres with thirty-one slaves. The most well-known of the slaves was Silvia, their seamstress, who sewed clothes for the other slaves and members of the family and wore a brightly-colored African turban.

During the December 1862 battle, with the Reynolds house located at the apex of the angle in the Confederate defensive line, the Southern commanders hoped the Union troops would advance into this zone and become caught in a devastating artillery crossfire. The Yankee troops avoided the "trap," leaving the battalion and the Rowan Artillery inactive.

Some interesting events that occurred at the Reynolds house later in the war bear mentioning. Eliza Reynolds, daughter of Dr. Reynolds, provided the following reminiscences:

> On May 17, 1864, the grounds of Lansdowne briefly became a battleground. Lieutenant John Latane of the Ninth Virginia Cavalry went on a scouting expedition to the rear of General Ulysses S. Grant's army. Lieutenant Latane and his cavalry got into a skirmish around the Reynolds house with the Union troops when he was accidentally shot by one of his own men. Too weak from loss of blood to be carried off by his men he was left under the care of Dr. Reynolds. On the same day, however, he was found by the enemy and taken to Lincoln Hospital in Washington, where he soon died of his wounds.

After the departure of Lieutenant Latane's detachment, Union troops thoroughly pillaged Dr. Reynolds's home. Eliza Reynolds recalled the details:

> They burned all the barns, carried off horses and all the cattle, setting the house on fire and smothering the flames with my father's books, thus saving the house. It is well known that my father, although too old for the service, was deeply interested in our [Confederate] cause and our men, so he was arrested with other gentlemen of the town and carried as a prisoner to Fort Delaware and my mother, our governess and we three children were left alone. A [Union] detachment led by their captain, who was intoxicated, he carried his pistol in his hand and demanded of my mother her keys and himself examined all locked places...cut into the beds and upholstered furniture as many hid their silver...At taps the soldiers returned to camp and as night came on, we took a few clothes and walked a mile or more to a neighbor's, one of our faithful servant men carrying my brother, a boy of twelve, who had cut his foot badly. The sticking plaster that my father had put over the cut had been torn off by the drunken captain, saying that he believed the boy a soldier. We remained with our good neighbors until we could cross the line and reach our grandfather's home in the town [Fredericksburg]....We found some of our furniture in the town where it had been taken from the deserted house...and a box of our books packed and ready to send off to Massachusetts—directed on the fly leaf of our family Bible to his mother by our [drunken] officer...and stating that the books had been captured from the Rebels.

While many Northern soldiers fought honorably for the cause of the Union, others saw the war as an opportunity to pillage and steal, destroying the very thing that their government advocated preserving. This devastation to land and property, as well as the northern economic advantages won by the war, sowed seeds of bitterness that would last for many years.

In 1862 Reilly's position at Lansdowne, held by General Longstreet's far right flank and General Jackson's far left flank, adjoining Hood's Division, fell almost exactly in the middle of the Confederate line. Amazingly, the Federals did not attack this part of the Confederate line, so Reilly's Battery was not engaged, but witnessed the dramatic spectacle of the Battle of Fredericksburg.

Colonel E. P. Alexander described the scene, with two enormous black observation balloons floating above the Federal line, as giving the view the appearance of a gigantic oil painting. Still men in blue stood in huge squares waiting to cross the river, while behind them immense columns of white-topped ambulances and wagons waited, interspaced by the dark blue squares of artillery batteries.

On December 13, Burnside launched over a dozen failed attacks on the Confederate line, primarily at Prospect Hill and Marye's Heights, resulting in staggering losses of thousands of Union men. That night, almost as a sign from the heavens, a rare and fantastic display of the aurora borealis appeared in full view. Imagine Old Tarantula, pacing the lines, cursing in his Irish accent and daring the enemy to attack him so he could fire his guns and destroy more Yankees.

CHAPTER V

CAMP LIFE, BATTLEFIELDS AND ARMY POLITICS

After this tremendous victory the Army of Northern Virginia moved into its winter encampment in the Rappahannock River valley. During the entire month of January 1863, heavy snowfall prevented active campaigning and provided a source of never-ending entertainment and diversion for the Confederate troops.

Between General Longstreet's winter headquarters and Forest Hill stood the campsite of General Hood's Texas Brigade. Every morning Longstreet had to pass through a barrage of snowballs, thrown by the fun-loving Texans. He endured this joke for several days until one morning he saw a group of soldiers lined up with snowballs in hand. He rode up to them and exclaimed, "Throw your snowballs, men, if you want to as much as you please. But if one of them touches me, not a man in this brigade shall have a furlough this winter. Remember that." Needless to say, Longstreet remained untouched.

The Great Snowball Fight of 1863 pitted Hood's Texans against General "Tighe" Anderson's Georgia Brigade. With haversacks full of snowballs, the mounted officers formed up in front of their commands. Battle flags flapping in the breeze and drums and bugles sounding, the one thousand five hundred man Texas Brigade attacked the Georgians. Leading one contingent of the Texas Brigade against the Georgians was Captain Reilly. As a testament to his popularity, his horse was reported to have been so covered with snow that it was impossible to distinguish its color. Thousands of snowballs were tossed back and forth, and after a prolonged struggle, which lasted the better part of the day, Hood's Division emerged victorious, bringing the Great Snowball Fight of 1863 to a close.

The Federal army encamped only a few hundred yards away, separated from the Confederates by a stream about two hundred feet wide. The snowball fight was not the only endeavor that attracted their attention. It was not uncommon for the Federal bands to serenade the Rebels with such Union favorites as *Yankee Doodle; Tramp, Tramp, Tramp, The Boys are Marching*; and *The Battle Hymn of the Republic*. The Confederate musicians often returned the compliment with *Dixie, The Bonnie Blue Flag, The Girl I Left Behind Me,* and *Maryland, My Maryland*. On some occasions the bands of both sides combined their talents to provide an entertaining concert for both armies to enjoy. Although they served opposite sides of a divided country, they were all still Americans in their hearts.

The Rowan Artillery's battalion commander, Major Bushrod Washington Frobel, had requested a transfer to his old friend General Whiting's District of the Cape Fear at Wilmington, North Carolina, which included Fort Fisher. Frobel received his transfer in the winter of 1863, accompanied by a promotion to the rank of lieutenant colonel of artillery and engineering. He departed the Army of Northern Virginia in February to take up his duties at Wilmington. Later in the war, he would see engineering duties with the Army of Tennessee at Macon, Georgia and as chief siege engineer in the defense of Savannah, Georgia from the hated "Yankee devil," General William Tecumseh Sherman and his "barbarian horde."

The new battalion commander, Major Mathias Winston Henry, took command on February 21. Born at Bowling Green, Kentucky, in 1838, Henry graduated from West Point in 1861. As a captain in General Jeb Stuart's horse artillery, he had served with Major John "The Gallant" Pelham, a Calhoun County, Alabama native, who graduated with Henry in the West Point Class of 1861.

At the Battle of Fredericksburg, Pelham placed himself and his gun crew in great danger, firing into the advancing Union troops from an exposed position with a Napoleon gun. General Stuart ordered one gun from Captain Henry's battery to come to Pelham's aid. After Henry's Blakely gun fired one shot, it was quickly taken out of action by General Hunt's powerful artillery. Still Pelham and Henry would not give ground. When Stuart called upon Pelham twice to retire his Napoleon, the young major replied, "Tell the General I can hold my ground."

General Lee, observing Pelham's Napoleon in action from Telegraph Hill, reportedly asked to which battery the gun belonged. When told it was Pelham's, he replied, "It is glorious to see such courage in one so young." Interestingly, while Pelham received the praise, he later gave credit to Captain Henry for the refusal to retire, according to John Cheves Haskell, who later played an important part in the future of the Rowan Artillery. Having lost only two men, it was Captain Henry who justified staying in position on the Union flank. More than likely, it was this act which impressed General Lee and the high command enough to promote him to major and give him command of Frobel's battalion.

A little known anecdote tells of Major Pelham's encounter with Captain Lewis Guy Phillips of Her Majesty's Grenadier Guards Regiment. Phillips, on leave from his post on the Canadian border, had come to observe General Lee's army. The night before the battle, he and Major Pelham became friends, while conversing around the campfire. Phillips gave Pelham a narrow red and blue striped ribbon and told him that it was his good-luck necktie, bearing his regimental colors, and asked him to wear it in the battle and return it as a souvenir. Pelham, touched by this act of friendship, agreed to wear it as a band on his hat. After the battle he returned it to Phillips, slightly blackened and powder smoked.

During the war, the men of both armies encamped in large groups, usually packed together in small tents. The camps were littered with refuse, rubbish and decomposing food. Heaps of manure and offal added to the filth, producing bacteria and viruses which spread death and sickness through the armies like wildfire. Bowel disorders, chronic diarrhea and dysentery constantly plagued the troops. This scenario became the perfect breeding ground for a wide array of devastating diseases and disorders. Outbreaks of typhoid fever, measles, chicken pox, mumps, whooping cough, pneumonia, and malaria were common. Poor diet and exposure to the weather compounded these problems. More men lost their lives as a result of illness than in battle.

The sexual desires of the men of both armies were quenched by multitudes of prostitutes, causing widespread outbreaks of venereal diseases such as gonorrhea and syphilis. The common treatment of the day for such diseases was mercury, inspiring the expression, "a night with Venus was a month with Mercury." Many southern women were compelled to turn to intermittent prostitution to feed themselves and their young children, who were left without fathers to provide a means of support. The invading Yankees also burned many farms and homes, destroying all food and leaving the women and children without shelter and sustenance. Many of these women were called "the fallen doves."

On February 7, 1863, Reilly's Battery left their encampment near Fredericksburg en route to Richmond. By February 18, they arrived at Guinea Station. Here the batteries, guns and baggage were placed on flat rail cars, and the wagons and horses were driven to Richmond. This was no simple task. The very heavy gun tubes had to be removed from their carriages, strapped, and tied securely to the rail car beds. This kept the very valuable tubes safe from falling or rolling off the cars in transit. Special tripods with heavy chains, ropes and pulleys lifted and positioned the tubes, a very time consuming and labor intensive task for the Confederates. The southern rail system was not standardized like that of the North, and different gauge railroad tracks required constant transferring and reloading of men, supplies and equipment at several stations along the way. The cost in time and extra labor greatly hindered the efficient use of railroads by the army.

All field artillery batteries had to be extremely mobile, both in battle and on the march. This mobility required an abundant use of horses and wheeled vehicles. Artillery units were divided by the number of horses used to accomplish their duties. In the "horse artillery," all men, including cannoneers, were mounted. They maneuvered with, and were attached to, the cavalry. A battery of four to six guns required about one hundred and fifty to two hundred horses.

The "mounted artillery" accompanied the infantry. While some men rode, most of the cannoneers marched alongside the guns, which were pulled by horses. A mounted artillery battery of four to six guns required from one hundred twenty-five to one hundred fifty horses, depending on the number of guns. The Rowan Artillery classified as a mounted battery, consisting of six guns.

The care and feeding of artillery horses occupied much of the battery's attention. Ideally, each horse received a daily ration of fourteen pounds of hay and twelve pounds of grain, mainly oats, corn or barley. All horses had to be fed daily, even when encamped in one spot. The volume of grain, hay and water required was enormous. A battery might camp in the same place for weeks at a time, consuming thousands of pounds of feed each day. With well over eight hundred thousand horses and mules in the army, it is easy to understand how very wide swaths of farmland were picked clean by the armies.

By February 20, the Rowan Artillery encamped alongside the Petersburg Railroad, one mile south of Manchester, Virginia. On March 12, Captain Reilly exchanged two Dahlgren howitzers for two Napoleon guns. These Napoleon guns were most likely the iron Confederate model, styled and manufactured by the Tredegar Iron Works of Richmond.

The Rowan Artillery's corps commander, General James Longstreet, had been placed in command of the Department of Virginia and North Carolina, which encompassed an area stretching from Richmond south to Wilmington, North Carolina. According to instructions from President Davis, Longstreet was to protect Richmond and its approaches from the south and east. He had positioned two brigadier generals, D. H. Hill and W. H. C. Whiting, in North Carolina. With General Lee's army in critical need of food and forage, the untouched counties in eastern North Carolina and southeastern Virginia provided an abundance of supplies. Longstreet directed General Hill to keep the Federals at bay so that this much needed forage could be loaded on wagons and sent to Lee and the Army of Northern Virginia. Federal forces had already occupied New Bern and Washington, North Carolina, so General Longstreet sent artillery and infantry reinforcements to help strengthen Hill's forces.

The Rowan Artillery received orders to join Hill at the Confederate siege of Washington, North Carolina. By April 5, 1863 the battery boarded rail cars at Petersburg and traveled on the Weldon Railroad to Tarboro, North Carolina. They arrived in Tarboro on April 6, and the next day marched twenty-five miles and encamped near Greenville, North Carolina. On April 8, they marched an additional twenty miles and occupied a position in fortifications around Washington, assigned by General Hill's chief of artillery, Major John Cheves Haskell. Washington is located on the Pamlico River, just east of its confluence with the Tar River. The Confederates positioned themselves at Fort Hill on Hill's Point, downstream from Washington. There, twelve Confederate guns controlled the fifty to seventy-five foot heights. At Rodman's Point, another grouping of Confederate artillery consisted of one thirty-two-pound siege gun and a twelve-pound English-made Whitworth gun.

The Rowan Artillery expended one thousand and fifty-seven artillery rounds between April 10 and April 15, an average of one hundred seventy-six rounds per day. When the Federals under the command of General John G. Foster succeeded in getting boats up the river with supplies and reinforcements, General Hill considered further efforts to dislodge the Yankees impractical with the troops and means he had at hand.

During the Confederate siege of Washington, the Union had several gunboats heavily armed with large naval guns. Their weak point was that they were constructed of wood, forcing the Federals to keep them hidden behind a bridge to avoid destruction by the Confederate artillery. The bridge offered a degree of protection, until Major Haskell received two rifled Whitworth guns, manufactured by Sir Joseph Whitworth in Manchester, England. The Whitworth guns possessed excellent and accurate long range firing capacity. These guns were transported by rail to Tarboro, North Carolina under special orders from General Longstreet approved by General Lee. They were stationed at Fort Powhatan, Virginia as part of Captain John Lane's Battery C, Sumter, Georgia Artillery, 11th Battalion of Light Artillery. One of these guns burst during the siege. The other was returned to General Longstreet at Franklin, Virginia after the battle. These very expensive and rare guns were coveted by the Army of Northern Virginia.

Soon after Haskell received these guns, one of the Federal gunboats ventured out into the open river. Before the Yankees realized the danger, their boat was hit and capsized. Aboard one of the enemy boats was a calliope, which the Yankees played about suppertime. Many of the Confederates had never heard this instrument and were fascinated by it. For about two hours after the "concert," the Yankees shelled the Confederate position with little results.

General D. H. Hill thanked the officers and men of Captain Reilly's battery for their efficient service at the siege of Washington in a note printed in the *Carolina Watchman*:

April 15, 1863

Captain Reilly — Many thanks to you, your officers, and your noble men for their efficient service. Would that you were attached to my command. I know of no men I would be so glad to have with me. May you have as happy and successful career as you deserve to have.

Respectfully,
D.H. Hill, Major General

On April 16, 1863, the Rowan Artillery received orders to move to Suffolk, Virginia to help support General Longstreet's forces against the Union command of General John Peck. The battery left Washington, North Carolina and retraced their route to Tarboro, arriving on April 18. By April 21, the battery traveled on the Weldon Railroad to Franklin, Virginia, arriving on April 22. They left Franklin on April 26 and marched thirty miles to camp near Suffolk. On May 3, the battery moved into battle line position at Suffolk. This proved to be a very short and inactive battle for the Rowan Artillery. The battery only fired ten rounds from its twenty-pound Napoleon gun. When the battle ended, the battery returned to Franklin.

General Lee had directed General Longstreet to disengage from Suffolk and rejoin the Army of Northern Virginia at Fredericksburg. By May 4, Longstreet's troops crossed the Blackwater River en route to Richmond, Virginia. They rejoined the Army of Northern Virginia too late to participate in the Battle of Chancellorsville.

By January 26, 1863, General Burnside had been replaced as a result of his disastrous defeat at Fredericksburg. The new commander of the Army of the

Potomac, General Joseph Hooker, was known as "Fighting Joe" because of his aggressive leadership. Born in Hadley, Massachusetts, in 1814, Hooker had graduated from West Point in the Class of 1837. He served in the Seminole War and as a staff officer to General Zachary Taylor in the Mexican War. As commander of the Army of the Potomac, he faced General Lee at the small crossroads of Chancellorsville, Virginia.

The fighting there has been called "Lee's perfect battle," because through a series of audacious moves he was able to vanquish a much larger army. The famous flanking movement by General Stonewall Jackson during the late afternoon of May 2, caught the one-armed Union General O.O. Howard and his Eleventh Corps by complete surprise, throwing the Federal army into a panic greater than the "great skedaddle" at First Manassas.

Disaster confronted the Confederacy at the height of victory, when General Stonewall Jackson was accidentally shot by troops of the Eighteenth North Carolina under the command of Major John Decatur Barry. Major Barry of Wilmington, North Carolina regretted this act for the rest of his short life. Barry died in March 1867 and was buried at Oakdale Cemetery in Wilmington, North Carolina.

About nine o'clock on the night of May 2, while trying to regroup and organize the Confederate lines, Jackson, clad in a black raincoat, and his staff were mistaken for a Federal scouting party and fired on by the North Carolinians. Jackson was hit three times, in the left upper arm, the left forearm and the right wrist. Doctors amputated his left arm that evening and moved him by ambulance twenty-seven miles to Guinea Station. Within days Jackson came down with pneumonia and succumbed on May 10, 1863. Visibly shaken, General Lee told his officers, "General Jackson lost his left arm, but I have lost my right arm." This quote would prove prophetic as the war progressed.

Lee's General Orders, No. 61 on May 11, 1863, announcing Jackson's death to the army, read:

With deep grief the Commanding General announces to the army the death of Lieut.-Gen. T. J. Jackson, who expired on the 10th inst. at 3 p.m. The daring, skill, and energy of this great and good soldier, by the decree of an All Wise Providence, are now lost to us.

But while we mourn his death we feel that his spirit still lives, and will inspire the whole army with his indomitable courage, and unshaken confidence in God as our hope and strength. Let his name be a watchword to his corps who have followed him to victory on so many fields. Let his officers and soldiers emulate his invincible determination to do everything in the defense of our beloved country.

By the time General Longstreet rejoined the Army of Northern Virginia, President Davis and the War Department had approved General Lee's request to make a second thrust into "Yankee Land." The Army of Northern Virginia began to organize their line of march northward by June 4. The Rowan Artillery traveled through Petersburg, Manchester, and Louisa Court House to camp near Culpeper Court House, Virginia. They crossed the Potomac River and marched twenty miles to Greencastle, Pennsylvania, arriving on June 26. From Greencastle they passed through Chambersburg, encamping two miles from the city.

During this march into northern territory, General Lee began to reorganize the command structure. Following Jackson's death, the army had three corps: the First Corps under General James Longstreet, the Second Corps under General Richard Ewell and the Third Corps under General A. P. Hill.

Each corps had its own chief of artillery, who along with battalion and battery commanders, reported to the chief of artillery for the Army of Northern Virginia, General William Nelson Pendleton. The new organization allowed greater advantages in firepower and opened the window to more officer positions and promotions. In an attempt to appease and reduce the tension surrounding the promotion situations of Captain Reilly and other artillery officers, General Lee issued Special Order Number 154 to his chief of artillery, General Pendleton, reading as follows:

June 8, 1863
Headqrs., Dept. of Northern Virginia

A board to consist of not less than three nor more than six artillery officers, to be designated by the Chief of Artillery, Army of Northern Virginia, will meet on the 1st of each month, or as soon thereafter as practicable, to report such facts in regard to the artillery and projectiles in use in this army as may come to their knowledge, and to make any suggestions in regard to changes and improvements they may think necessary, and also to make tables of ranges of guns for the use of the Confederate States Artillery.

General Pendleton replied to this on June 15, 1863, in the following words:

In obedience to special orders No. 154, Headquarters, Department of North Virginia, June 8, the following named officers are designated to constitute the board there named, viz:

Col. E. P. Alexander, President; Major Dearing; Major Henry; Captain Reilly, Henry's Battalion; Captain Blount, Dearing's Battalion; Captain Fraser, Cabell's Battalion.

The Board will be called together by the president on the earliest day practicable, and will proceed to discharge the duties indicated in the order, and will report the result within the present week if practicable, or as soon as may be.

During this time Major Winston Henry applied for a transfer to the western theater and began to groom Major John C. Haskell, former chief of artillery to General D.H. Hill, to take command of his battalion, which included the Rowan Artillery. John Cheves Haskell was born in 1841 at Abbeville, South Carolina and attended South Carolina College, now the University of South Carolina in Columbia. His four brothers also served as officers in the Army of Northern Virginia. The Haskells were a large and powerful family and part of the southern aristocracy.

The following events, which took place during the Battle of Gaines' Mill, where Haskell served as volunteer aide de camp to General Longstreet, provide insight into the character of this extremely brave young Confederate major. As Haskell described his experiences:

When we got close to the enemy line, we found a great many men lying down. My men followed suit, and I set to work trying to push them in. I saw a stand of colors held upright by a color bearer lying flat on his face. I rode to him and jerked it out of his hands. He at once jumped up and demanded them back, saying in reply to my question that he would take them in if the colonel, and he pointed to him lying near, would go on.

I rode over to the colonel and punched him in the back with the flagstaff. He jumped up, but when I told him to take the colors and lead his men in, he set to shaking as if in a chill, and suddenly broke off in a run to the rear. I shifted the flag to my left hand and riding up to him, struck him on the head with my sword; but it turned and the flat of it struck him hard enough to knock him to his knees. He cried out but ran on some thirty yards, when he jumped in the air and fell, apparently dead.

Almost immediately after a ball struck my saddle, grazing my leg and going into my horse, which fell to his knees. He had, up to this time, been the best horse I ever saw in

71

battle, the only effect of the firing being to steady him, though I thought he would be utterly unmanageable. I pulled him to his feet, and — not realizing that he fell from the shot — struck my spurs to him. When the spurs pricked him, though I am sure he was mortally wounded, he made one of his typical rushes and had me over the breastworks. But he was shot dead in the act of leaping, and I was lying under him among the enemy.

A captain, I think of a New York regiment, ran up to me and grabbing the flagstaff called out to me, "You damned little rebel, surrender." I held on and jerked him to me, striking at him at the same time with my sword, which was hung to my wrist by a sword knot. He at once jumped back and fired at me with his pistol, cursing me all the time and tugging at the flagstaff. I kept jerking it back and striking at him with my sword, while at the same time struggling to get from under my dead horse, which was lying on my legs.

One ball from the pistol struck the star of my collar and burned my neck like fire, while another struck my little finger, breaking it and smashing a seal ring which I wore. Another just grazed my leg, but that one felt like a double-heated, hot iron, and made me struggle so that I found myself free from my horse and on my feet.

Our troops by this time were pouring in and the Yankees running, my opponent among them. But he was a little too late, and I caught up with him. I cut down on him with both hands, expecting to split him as we used to read of in novels, but my sword bounced off, knocking him to his knees. He rose and turned, facing me with his pistol in his hand. I never doubted but that he was about to shoot again and ran him through.

General Hood, reforming his troops, approached on Major Haskell's left. Hood noticed how bloody Haskell was and asked if he was seriously hurt. Major Haskell replied that he was not. Hood then suggested that Haskell and his men join other Confederate troops to attack the enemy position and gun emplacements on the right. As Haskell later described:

I did so, and we charged across the plateau about four or five hundred feet. When I got within a few feet of the guns, I marked a gunner fixing his lanyard into the friction primer. I made a run to cut him down before he could fire, but he was too quick. When I was not over ten feet from the muzzle, the gun went off. The shot struck my right arm, crushing it and tearing it off at the shoulder. When it hit me, it seemed to knock me up in the air and spin me around two or three times, though I suppose that was imaginary, and then dashed me down with a force that knocked all the breath out of me.

When I came to, I found my arm wrapped around my sword blade in a most remarkable manner. I sat up, but almost immediately everything went dark, and I supposed I was dying. After some time I regained consciousness and unwound the fragments of my arm from the sword blade, which I got back into the scabbard. I succeeded in stuffing my arm into the breast of my coat, got to my feet and started to the rear using a flagstaff as a support.

As Haskell struggled to get help, he fell and could not get up. Just as he expected to die, General Whiting came riding by and, seeing Haskell, dismounted and gave him some whiskey from his flask. General Whiting, with the assistance of a straggler, helped Haskell onto his horse and accompanied him to a field hospital. The surgeon attended to Haskell's wounds, bandaging the site of the amputation tightly to his body. Then Whiting turned Haskell over to a member of his staff, Colonel Upson from Texas.

Proceeding to the rear of the Confederate lines, Haskell passed General "Marse Robert" Lee and his staff. Seeing his condition, Lee had a private ambulance brought up to take Haskell to the hospital in Richmond for further care. Before Haskell left, General Longstreet had his medical director, Colonel D'Orsay Cullen, examine him. Seeing that he was suffering greatly, Cullen placed some bitter powder in Haskell's mouth. He told Haskell after his recovery that he had given him enough morphine to kill several men to allow him to die easily. Colonel Cullen often said that Haskell's recovery from his medicine was much more remarkable than his recovery from his wounds. Taken to Richmond, Haskell recovered under the care of Thomas Dudley and his family.

By June 8, 1863, Major Haskell had recovered sufficiently to rejoin the army and was assigned to Major Henry's battalion. Although Major Henry was Haskell's junior by date of commission, General Longstreet advised Haskell not to assume command until Henry had left the Army of Northern Virginia. The two young officers divided the command without any difficulty or disagreement in the spirit of true southern gentlemen.

For Captain Reilly, learning of Major Henry's request for a transfer and the placement of Major Haskell to assume command of the battalion was like rubbing salt into an already festering wound. His "Irish" was up and rightfully so. He was continually passed over for promotions.

By the end of May 1863, General Pendleton received and considered an application for Reilly's promotion. He ruled that it could not be approved at that time because there were already nineteen active majors of artillery and existing regulations only authorized seventeen. Even though Captain Reilly's promotion was temporarily blocked, the door remained open to him in the person of the governor of North Carolina, Zebulon Vance.

Governor Vance did not like President Davis and the two men had many disagreements. Vance expressed constant concerns that North Carolina troops, serving outside the state, would be passed over for promotions in favor of men from other states, especially Virginia. To counter this possibility, he claimed the right to promote company and field-grade officers among North Carolina regiments created prior to the Confederate Conscription Act of 1862. The Rowan Artillery, officially the Tenth North Carolina Company D, First State Regiment of Artillery, fell into this category. Governor Vance conceded to the Confederate government the authority over promotions of conscript troops, but contended that the law creating the original regiments gave him the sole right for appointments and promotions of their officers, and that he still had that right.

The Confederate government, on the other hand, maintained that this authority passed to them when state troops entered Confederate service. This dispute gave officers of the early North Carolina regiments two avenues to promotions, the government and president of the Confederate States of America and the governor of the state of North Carolina. Sometimes an officer could be caught in between these two authorities, each expecting the other to act. Political and other influential contacts could resolve these uncertainties, but this took time. Reilly was now among those caught in the web of uncertainty.

General Whiting, now commander of the Cape Fear defenses, came to the aid of his old friend, Captain Reilly. Although he was well aware of these conflicting views, he had sponsored Reilly for promotion since the beginning of the war. On May 30, 1863, he penned a long letter to Governor Vance, which traced in detail and with considerable praise Reilly's military career in both the United States and the Confederate service. He noted Reilly's eminent claims to promotion, "not only for length of service, many juniors having been promoted over him with not a tenth of his claim, but for signal skill and the most distinguished service on many battle fields," adding that "he has been repeatedly recommended by Generals J. E. Johnston, G. W. Smith and myself." Whiting continued that, "during his whole service the perfection of his battery in skill, discipline, efficiency to the minutest details, has been the pride of his commanders and the remark of all inspectors." In summation, he added, "I do not detract from others when I say I would rather have Reilly's Battery than any other in the Confederate States." Whiting concluded by recommending that "Capt. Reilly be advanced to the grade of lieutenant colonel and refer to Gen. Lee, Lt. Gen. Longstreet, Maj. Gen. Hood and Brigadier Gen. Law."

In a separate letter to Governor Vance on the same date, Major B. W. Frobel,

Whiting's chief of artillery and Reilly's immediate superior after the Seven Days, added his praise of Old Tarantula. Frobel traced his actions through Freeman's Ford, Thoroughfare Gap and Second Manassas, where "the skill and daring with which he handled his guns contributed in an eminent degree to the success of our armies on the glorious 30th of August." He continued by citing the excellence of Reilly's service at Boonsborough and at Sharpsburg, noting that at the withdrawal from the latter, Reilly's Battery covered the rear and was the last to cross the river." Frobel concluded by saying that through personal association, he knew Reilly to be "an able, efficient and gallant officer, and as an artillery officer surpassed by none." To these recommendations General D. H. Hill added warm praise and compliments for the conduct of Reilly's Battery at the Siege of Washington, North Carolina.

Major James Reilly
Taken from portrait at the Cape Fear Museum, Wilmington, NC

Captain John A. Ramsay
Courtesy of the North Carolina Department of Archives

Firing on *Star of the West*; *The Citadel Archives & Museum*

George E. Haynsworth
The Citadel Archives & Museum

78

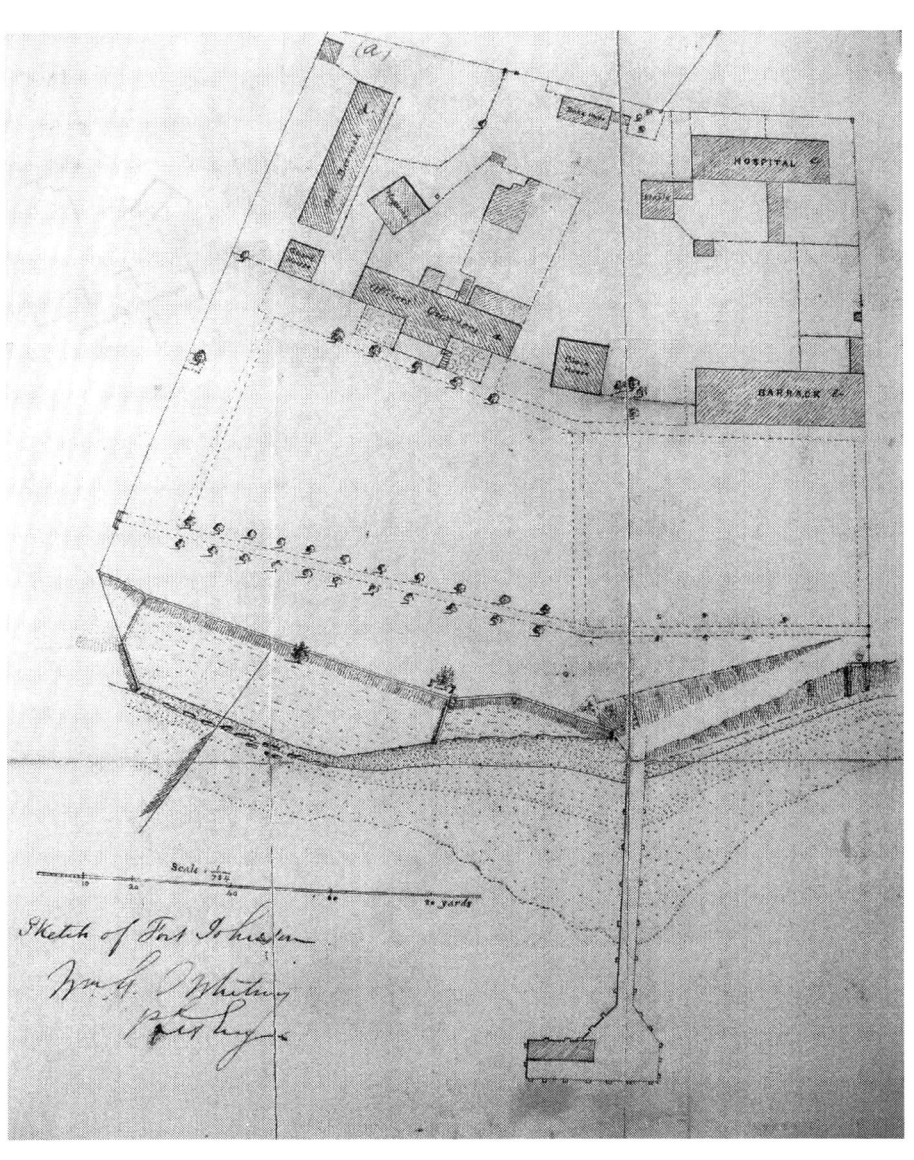

Never before published sketch of Fort Johnston by Lt. William Whiting, 1856
Photo courtesy of the City of Southport, NC

The old Ramsay Homestead, Iredell County, North Carolina
Photo courtesy John E. Ramsay

Colonel James B. Walton, Chief of Artillery, First Corps until Gettysburg, 1863.
Photo courtesy of Louisiana State Museum

Major Mathias W. Henry in West Point cadet uniform, Battalion Commander
Photo courtesy United States Military Academy, West Point

Colonel John Cheves Haskell, Battalion Commander. Please note Haskell has arranged his empty right sleeve so as to give the impression that his arm is still there.
Photo courtesy Library of Congress

General Joseph Eggleston Johnston
Photo: generalsandbrevets.com

General Robert E. Lee, "Marse Robert"
Photo: generalsandbrevets.com

General James Longstreet, "Old Pete"
Photo: generalsandbrevets.com

General Thomas Jonathan Jackson,
"Stonewall" *Photo: generalsandbrevets.com*

General John B. Magruder, "The Prince"
Photo: generalsandbrevets.com

General Daniel Harvey Hill
Photo: generalsandbrevets.com

General Ambrose Powell Hill
Photo: generalsandbrevets.com

General Richard Stoddert Ewell, "Old
Baldy "*Photo: generalsandbrevets.com*

General John Bell Hood
Photo: generalsandbrevets.com

General James Ewell Brown Stuart, "Jeb"
Photo: generalsandbrevets.com

General William Henry Chase Whiting,
"Little Billy"
Photo: generalsandbrevets.com

General Braxton Bragg
Photo: generalsandbrevets.com

General William Nelson Pendleton,
Chief of Artillery, Army of Northern Virginia
Photo: generalsandbrevets.com

General Edward Porter Alexander,
Chief of Artillery, First Corps after Gettys-
berg, 1863 *Photo: generalsandbrevets.com*

General Armistad Lindsay Long
Chief of Artillery, Second Corps
Photo: generalsandbrevets.com

General Reuben Lindsay Walker,
Chief of Artillery, Third Corps
Photo: generalsandbrevets.com

General Henry Jackson Hunt,
Chief of Artillery, Union Army of the Potomac, " The Artillery Fox"
Photo: generalsandbrevets.com

Union General John Pope
Photo: generalsandbrevets.com

Union General Ambrose Everett Burnside
Photo: generalsandbrevets.com

Union General George Brinton McClellan,
"Little Mac"
Photo: generalsandbrevets.com

Union General Joseph Hooker
Photo: generalsandbrevets.com

Union General Ulysses Simpson Grant,
"The Butcher"
Photo: generalsandbrevets.com

Union General George Gordon Meade,
"The Snapping Turtle"
Photo: generalsandbrevets.com

Union General Benjamin Franklin Butler,
"The Beast," "Spoons"
Photo: generalsandbrevets.com

Admiral David Dixon Porter,
Union Commander, Fort Fisher fleet
Courtesy of National Archives

Major James Hoffman Hill
*Courtesy New Hanover Public Library,
Wilmington, NC*

Captain Alfred Crippen VanBenthuysen
*Courtesy of the Ralph W. Donnelly papers,
Marine Corps History Center*

Union Captain E. Lewis Moore,
Assistant Adjutant General Volunteers,
Abbott's Brigade Seventh Connecticut
Courtesy of David M. Moore, DVM
(Great-grandson)

Unidentified soldier holding the Seventh
Connecticut flag used at Fort Fisher,
North Carolina
Courtesy of David M. Moore, DVM
(great-grandson)

Union Captain J. Homer Edgerly
History of The Third New Hampshire, by Captain Daniel Eldredge

Captain Robert T. Chapman, CSS Sumter
Library of Congress

Union General Adelbert Ames
United States Army Miiltary Historical Institute. (USAMHI)

Union Commander James Parker
USAMHI

Union General Curtis and Colonel Lamb, CSA at Curtis' New York home post war.
Photo courtesy College of William & Mary

British Armstrong gun. Please note brass disk used to adjust braking calipers.
Courtesy of Fort Fisher Historic Site

Left: Union Lt. Commander Kidder Randolph Breese. *Library of Congress*

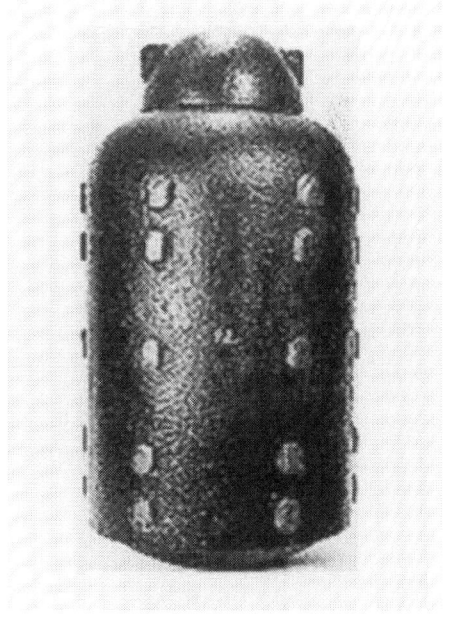

150 pound British Armstrong Shell
Library of Congress

Battery Buchanan at Fort Fisher where Major Reilly held out until the end. *Library of Congress*

Shepard's Battery where Major Reilly was in command during the second Union attack on Fort Fisher. *Library of Congress*

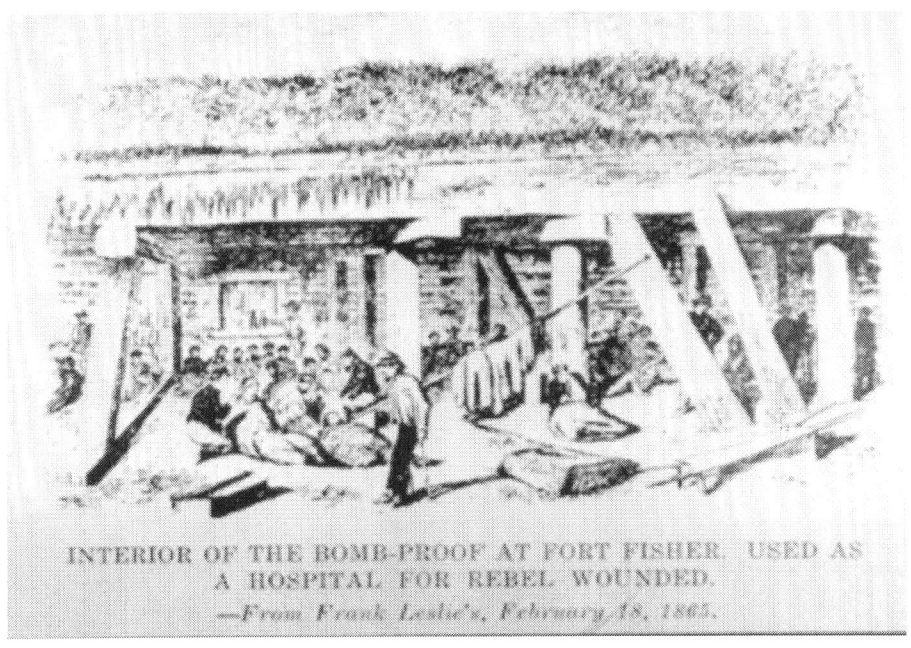

INTERIOR OF THE BOMB-PROOF AT FORT FISHER, USED AS
A HOSPITAL FOR REBEL WOUNDED.
—From Frank Leslie's, February 18, 1865.

Interior of Hospital Bombproof where Lamb and Whiting were taken after they were
wounded after the second attack on Fort Fisher.
From Frank Leslie's Photo, Library of Congress

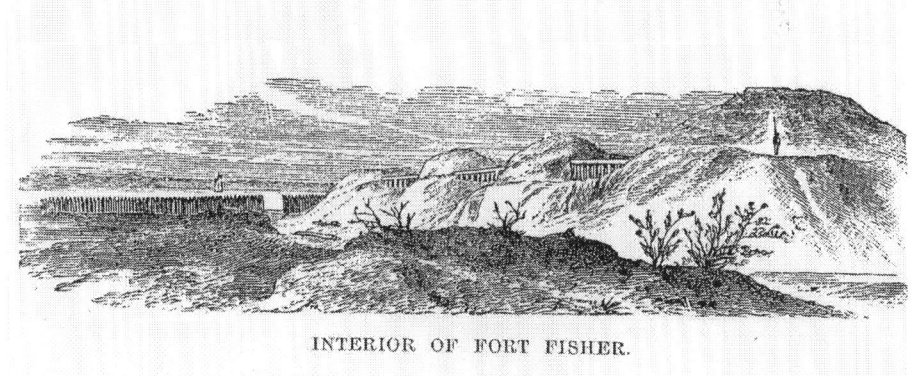

INTERIOR OF FORT FISHER.

Interior of Fort Fisher showing the sallyport overlooking the Cape Fear River.
Courtesy Fort Fisher Historic Site

Chesapeake Hospital near Fort Monroe, Virginia was for officers only. This is where Union General Curtis and Colonel Lamb, CSA were recuperating and established their lifelong friendship.
CivilWarPhotos.net/

Union General George Armstrong Custer, "Auntie," "Fanny," "Curly," stole Huger's spurs.
Photo: generalsandbrevets.com

Colonel Frank Huger, CSA, post war
Courtesy United States Military Academy

Ramsay's Battery being overrun and all guns captured by Union Cavalry under General Henry Davis at Paineville, Virginia April 5, 1865.
Sketch by Alfred Waud, Library of Congress

One of Captain Lampkin's Confederate iron mortars placed on the town square at Amelia Court House, Virginia. *Courtesy of Chris Clarkins, Historian, Petersburg National Battlefield*

Captain John A. Ramsay, post war
Photo courtesy of John E. Ramsay

Margaret Beal Ramsay (Maggie). It is possible that she is holding the family Bible.Circa 1876-1880
Photo courtesy of John E. Ramsay

First Presbyterian Church, built 1826, Salisbury, North Carolina.
Photo courtesy John E. Ramsay

The interior of the First Presbyterian Church of Salisbury, North Carolina, built in 1826. This picture was taken about 1890. John A. Ramsay is a deacon sitting 4th from left on the front row.

Photo courtesy John E. Ramsay

John A. Ramsay, state senator from
Rowan County, North Carolina,1897.
A gifted public servant.
Courtesy of NC Department of Archives,
Raleigh, NC

John A. Ramsay circa 1900-1910. An
honorable Confederate veteran.
Courtesy John E. Ramsay

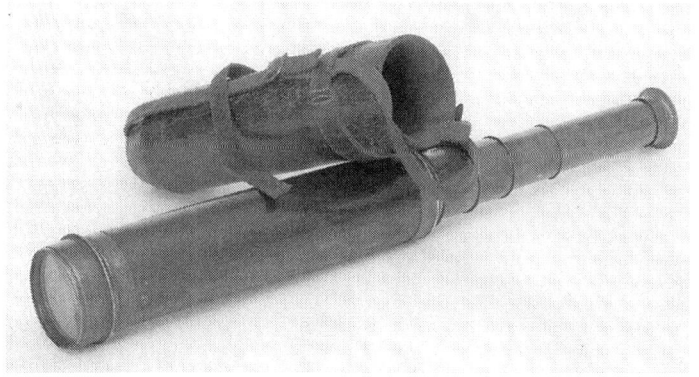

Captain Ramsay's telescope made by McAllisler and Brother of Philadelphia, Pennsylvania. *Courtesy of John E. Ramsay*

John Andrew Ramsay's telescope and sword placed on his tombstone at Chestnut Hill Cemetery, Salisbury, North Carolina. *Author's photo*

Post-1924 photo of the Confederate Statue in downtown Wilmington, North Carolina. Ramsay's son was the model for the statue's face. *Courtesy Lower Cape Fear Historical Society*

Reilly's National Association Veteran's Mexican War Shield presented to him for his gallant service in the Mexican War.
Photograph Courtesy of War Time Collectibles/ Mr. Lipps of Camden, SC

Major James Reilly's house located at 111 South Sixth Street, Wilmington, North Carolina, where the family resided until 1883. *Author's photo*

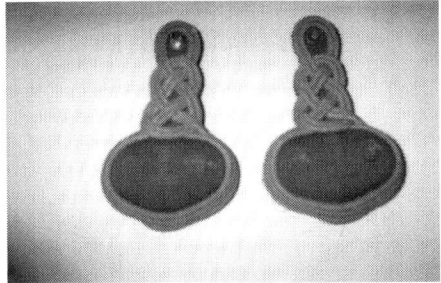

Major Reilly's artillery epaulets
Photo courtesy of Dr. James Reilly Lee

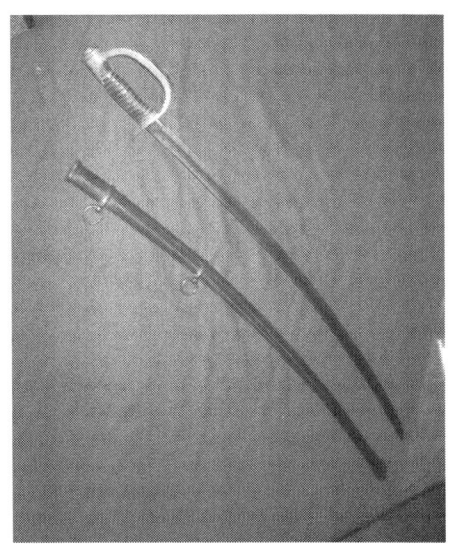

Major Reilly's sword used at surrender of
Fort Fisher. *Courtesy of Fort Fisher State
Historic Site*

The distinguished looking Major James
Reilly, post war, "Old Tarantula."
Courtesy of Mr. Lawrence Lee

107

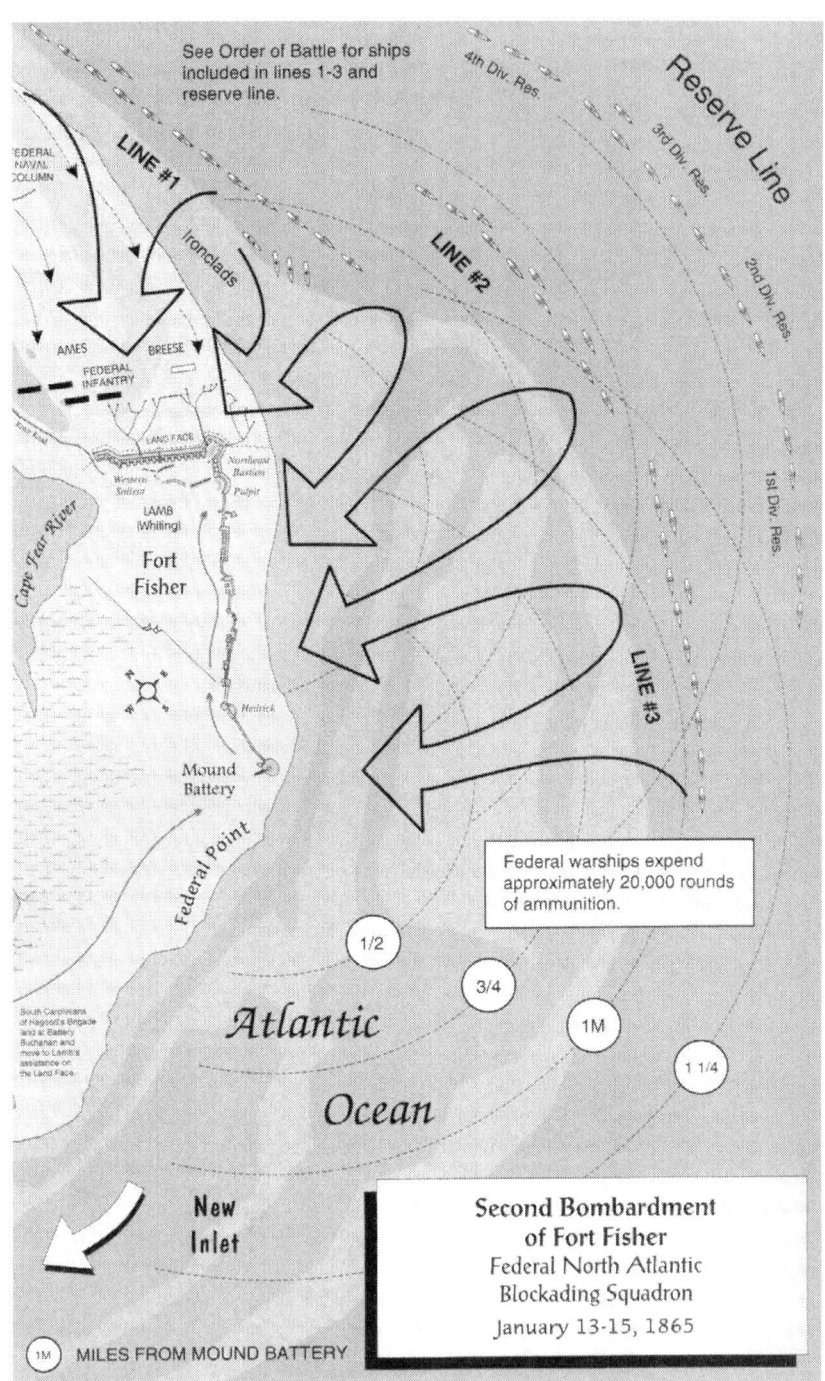

See Order of Battle for ships included in lines 1-3 and reserve line.

Reserve Line

4th Div. Res

3rd Div. Res

2nd Div. Res.

1st Div. Res.

LINE #1

LINE #2

LINE #3

FEDERAL NAVAL COLUMN

Ironclads

AMES

BREESE

FEDERAL INFANTRY

LAND FACE

Northeast Bastion

Western Sallent

Pulpit

LAMB (Whiting)

Fort Fisher

Cape Fear River

Hedrick

Mound Battery

Federal Point

Federal warships expend approximately 20,000 rounds of ammunition.

1/2

3/4

1M

1 1/4

Atlantic

Ocean

South Carolinians of Hagood's Brigade land at Battery Buchanan and move to Lamb's assistance on the Land Face.

New Inlet

Second Bombardment of Fort Fisher
Federal North Atlantic
Blockading Squadron
January 13-15, 1865

1M   MILES FROM MOUND BATTERY

Second Bombardment of Fort Fisher
Map courtesy Mark A. Moore from his book Moore's Historical Guide to The Wilmington Campaign and the Battles for Fort Fisher

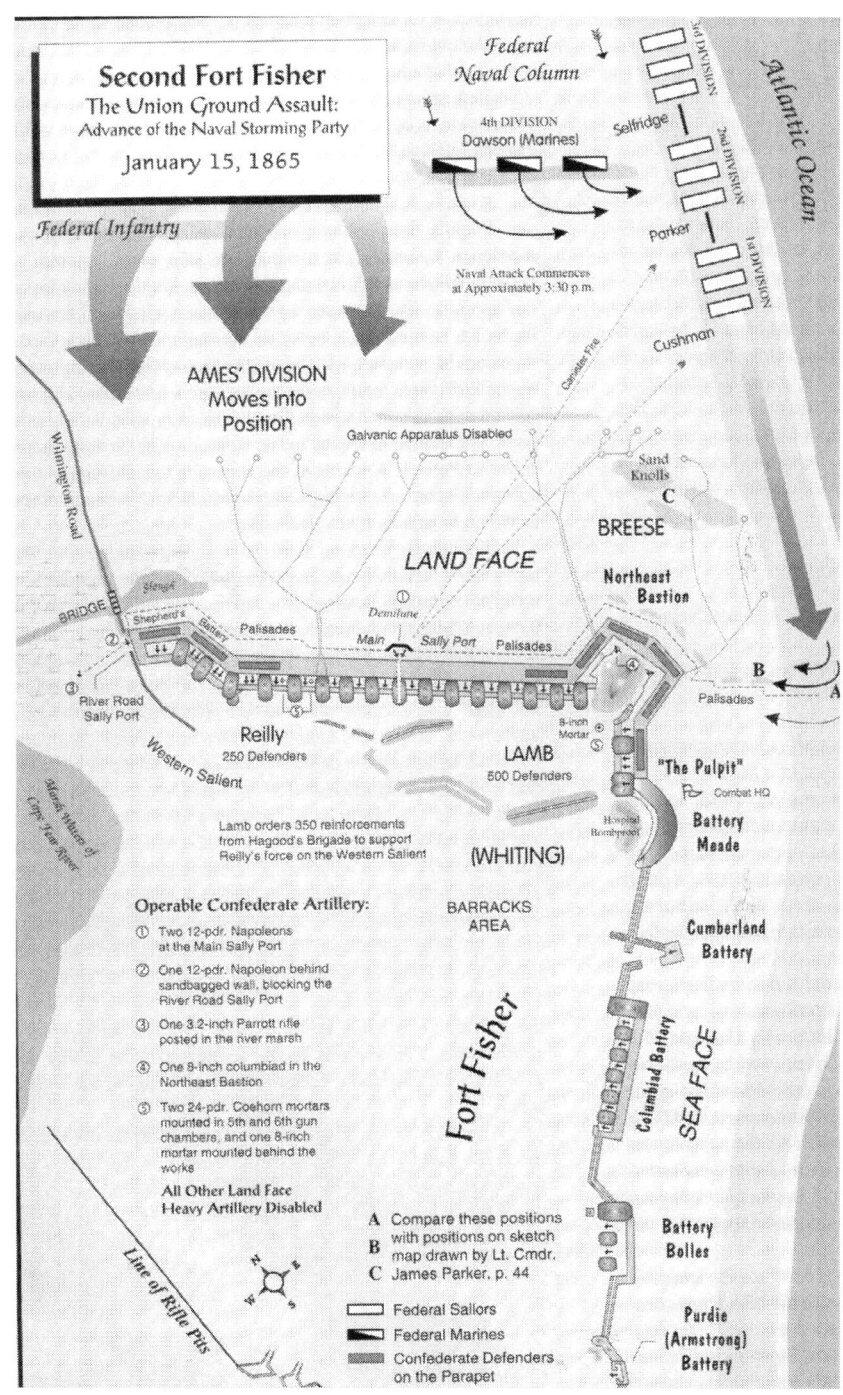

Second Fort Fisher

The Union Ground Assault:
Advance of the Naval Storming Party

January 15, 1865

Federal Naval Column

4th DIVISION
Dawson (Marines)

Selfridge

Parker

Naval Attack Commences
at Approximately 3:30 p.m.

Atlantic Ocean

2nd DIVISION

1st DIVISION

Federal Infantry

Cushman

AMES' DIVISION
Moves into
Position

Galvanic Apparatus Disabled

Sand
Knolls

C

BREESE

Wilmington Road

LAND FACE

Northeast
Bastion

Siege 4

Shepherd's

Battery

Palisades

Demilune

Main   Sally Port   Palisades

BRIDGE

B

River Road
Sally Port

8-inch
Mortar

Palisades

A

Reilly
250 Defenders

Western Salient

LAMB
600 Defenders

"The Pulpit"

Combat HQ

Lamb orders 350 reinforcements
from Hagood's Brigade to support
Reilly's force on the Western Salient

Hospital
Bombproof

(WHITING)

Battery
Meade

Marsh Shore of Cape Fear River

Operable Confederate Artillery:

① Two 12-pdr. Napoleons
at the Main Sally Port

② One 12-pdr. Napoleon behind
sandbagged wall, blocking the
River Road Sally Port

③ One 3.2-inch Parrott rifle
posted in the river marsh

④ One 8-inch columbiad in the
Northeast Bastion

⑤ Two 24-pdr. Coehorn mortars
mounted in 5th and 6th gun
chambers, and one 8-inch
mortar mounted behind the
works

All Other Land Face
Heavy Artillery Disabled

BARRACKS
AREA

Fort Fisher

Cumberland
Battery

Columbiad Battery

SEA FACE

A   Compare these positions
B   with positions on sketch
     map drawn by Lt. Cmdr.
C   James Parker, p. 44

□ Federal Sailors
◼ Federal Marines
▬ Confederate Defenders
    on the Parapet

Battery
Bolles

Purdie
(Armstrong)
Battery

Line of Rifle Pits

Map courtesy Mike A. Moore from his book Moore's Historical Guide to The Wilmington Campaign and the Battles for Fort Fisher

109

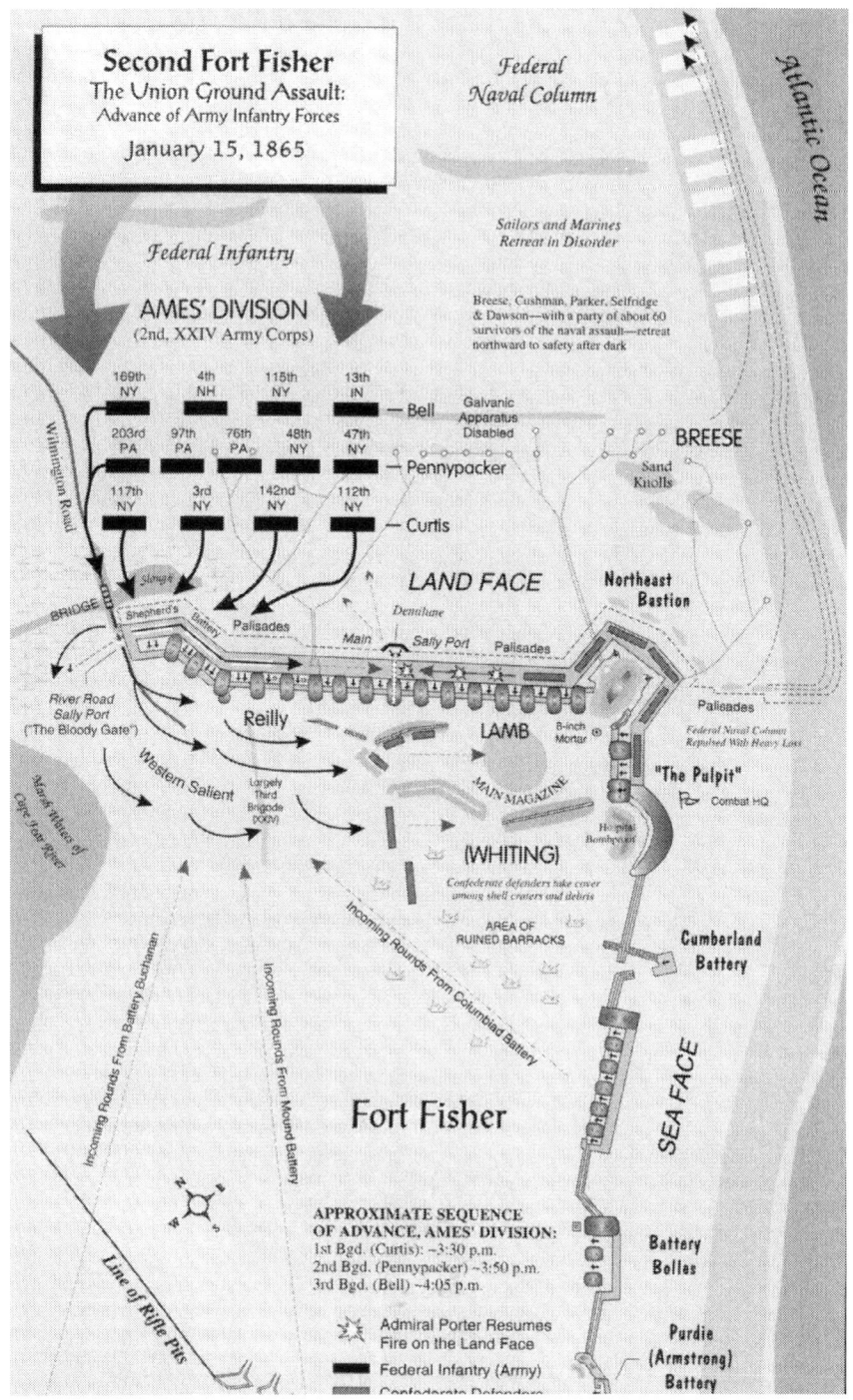

Map courtesy Mark A. Moore from his book Moore's Historical Guide to The Wilmington Camapaign and the Battles for Fort Fisher

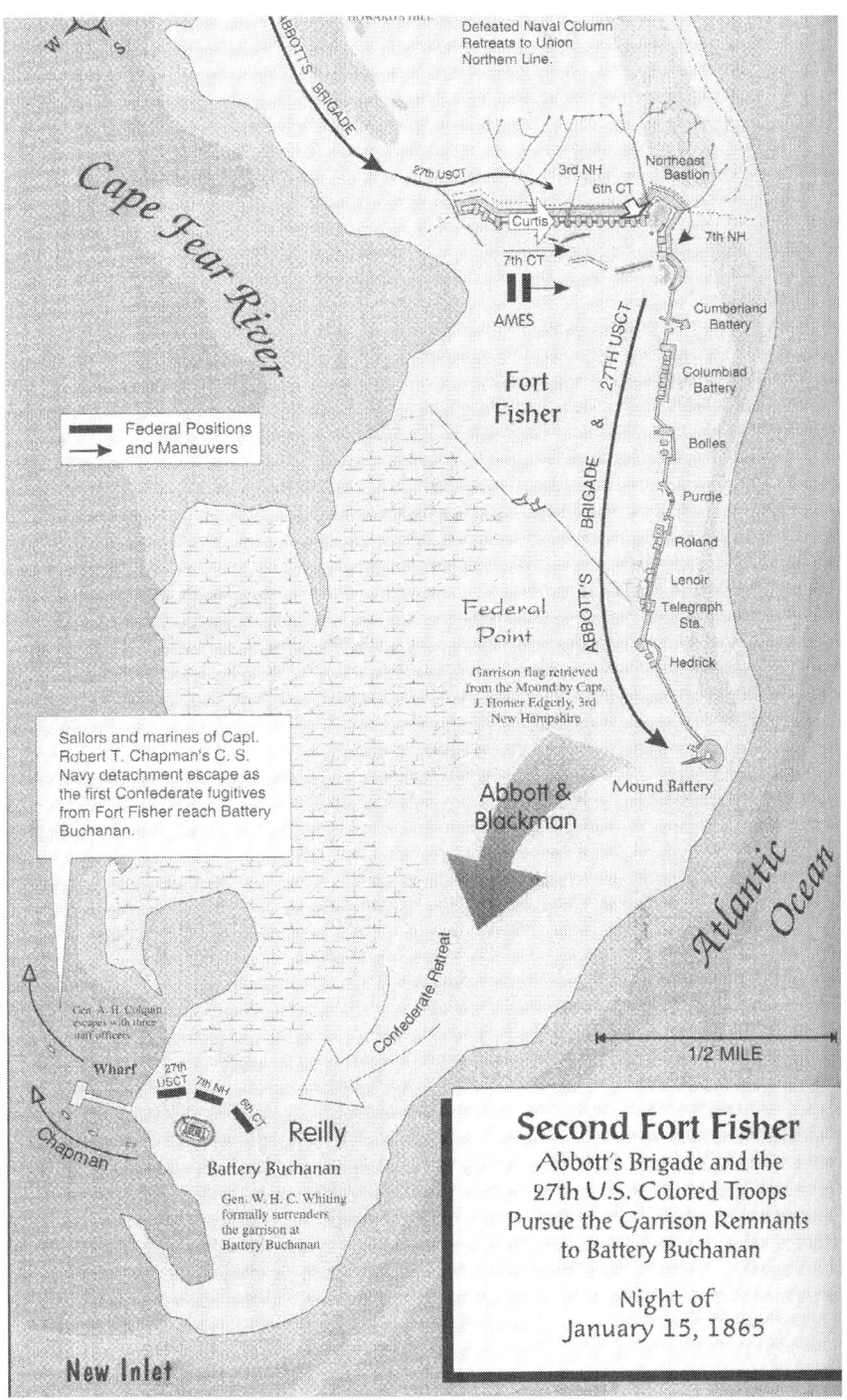

Map courtesy Mark A. Moore from his book Moore's Historical Guide to The Wilmington Camapaign and the Battles for Fort Fisher

Chapter VI

A Small Town Somewhere in Pennsylvania

During this period of military and political sparring over Captain Reilly's promotion, an epic battle in which Reilly's Battery would play a meaningful part loomed in the small Pennsylvania town of Gettysburg. After two decisive Confederate victories at Fredericksburg and Chancellorsville, General Lee decided to take the offense to draw the Federal army away from Washington and destroy it, or to position the Army of Northern Virginia between the Union army and the northern capital, giving the Confederate States the power to negotiate for their independence. A victory on northern soil might also attract much needed European support for the southern cause. In addition, marching into the fertile farm lands of Pennsylvania could supply the Confederate army with necessary food for the troops and fodder and grain for the large number of horses and mules.

Gettysburg was the county seat of Adams County, with a population of two thousand four hundred people. Situated among gently undulating, lush rolling farmlands, the town was surrounded by a patchwork of grain fields, pastures, orchards and woods, as well as two rocky, granite hills south of town known as Little and Big Round Top. During the war, Little Round Top was owned by two men, Ephriam Hanaway, who had thirty acres on the western face, and Jacob Weikerk, who owned the eastern face. Gettysburg was also home to Pennsylvania College and a Lutheran Seminary. It served as a major hub of over ten roads, leading to Baltimore and surrounding smaller cities, including York, Chambersburg, Carlisle, Emmitsburg and Hagerstown. Gettysburg also boasted a good railroad system.

As the Army of Northern Virginia moved north, the men of the Rowan Artillery sensed that great danger was in the air and that the angels of death would soon be engaged in another heroic struggle. Captain Reilly had organized an association for the spiritual welfare of his men to remind them of the efficacy of prayer before going into battle. Lieutenant Ramsay read his personal King James Bible throughout the war. Many times as he read his favorite psalm, the ninety-first, these words gave him peace of mind and encouragement, "He that dwelleth in the secret place of the most High shall abide under the shadow of the Almighty." Another verse in this chapter promised, "He shall cover thee with his feathers, and under His wings shalt thou trust. A thousand shall fall at thy side...but it shall not come nigh thee." The power of prayer must have kept both of these men in God's hands. Amazingly, they both survived the war without any severe injury or wound, a remarkable feat considering the many bloody artillery battles in which they participated.

Saturday, June 27, 1863, found Reilly's Battery encamped two miles from Chambersburg in a little settlement called Snickersville at the foot of the mountains. The First Corps, commanded by General Longstreet, to which the Rowan Artillery was attached, rested there until June 30. The Army of Northern Virginia was penetrating deep into Yankee territory. About this time General Lee received word that Lincoln had replaced General Hooker with General George Meade, who ordered the Union army across the Potomac, and headed northward.

Major General George G. Meade was born in 1815 in Cadiz, Spain to a wealthy Philadelphia family. He ranked nineteenth out of fifty-six in his graduating class of 1835 at West Point and served in the Seminole and Mexican Wars. Hearing of Meade's appointment, General Lee knew he could not afford to have his army scattered around the Pennsylvania countryside. He decided to unite his army east of the mountains and with his staff searched the maps for a convenient location to concentrate. After careful study and consultation, he chose the town of Gettysburg. On June 29, the day before Lee made this decision, General A. P. Hill had given permission to General Henry Heth to go into Gettysburg to investigate the rumor that a supply of shoes, much needed by the Army of Northern Virginia, was in the town.

General Heth sent a brigade to Gettysburg on June 30, to investigate the situation. They found that a three-thousand-man Federal cavalry force, commanded by General John Buford, had just occupied the town. The Confederate brigade did not attempt to attack the superior Union force. On July 1, the remainder of General Heth's command and General William D. Pender's twelve-thousand-man division arrived at Gettysburg. Aware of their advantage, the Confederate command took the offensive and so began the Battle of Gettysburg.

General John F. Reynolds and his Union First Corps arrived just in time to prevent the Confederates from taking the high ground, which Buford on his horse, "Gray Eagle," desperately tried to hold. Galloping forward on his horse, Fancy, General Reynolds was killed at McPherson's Wood by a single shot to the head. By now, both armies were rushing to the sound of battle. Great confusion was the order of the day. The Confederates pushed the Federals through the town. The Yankees retreated to Cemetery Hill and Culp's Hill, where they established a formidable defense. During the chaos of the day, Lee ordered General Richard S. Ewell to take Culp's and Cemetery Hills, if he found it practicable. Ewell was instructed to avoid a general engagement until the arrival of the other divisions of the army.

Ewell, mounted on his cherished horse, "Rifle," failed to seize the opportunity and did not follow up with an attack on Culp's Hill. As a result, the Federals maintained and reinforced this excellent line of defense, preparing for a possible Confederate attack the next day. Ewell's failure to take Culp's Hill is often considered Lee's lost opportunity. Generations of historians have speculated how the more aggressive Stonewall Jackson would have reacted to this situation, many proposing that Jackson would not have stopped until Culp's Hill was in Confederate hands.

The new commander of the Army of the Potomac, General Meade, riding his horse, "Baldy," did not want to fight at Gettysburg. His original plan called for a defensive position along the Pipe Creek Line, running approximately twenty miles, east to west, in northern Maryland. Topographically, the Pipe Creek Line was by far a superior defensive position, composed of a natural tangle of ridges and ravines with open fields running in front of very commanding heights. It presented an extremely unsuitable location for a Confederate offensive attack. Situated between the Army of Northern Virginia and Washington, it was serviced by excellent roads for Union troop movement. Hesitant to move his army with the Confederates so close, Meade decided to stay at Gettysburg and maintain a defensive position. This decision provided the advantage of high ground and interior lines, as well as a position between the Confederate army and Washington.

At four in the afternoon on Wednesday, July 1, 1863, the Rowan Artillery, as part of Henry's Battalion of the First Corps, left their camp at Greenwood and marched thirteen miles to bivouac at Marsh Creek, just four miles west of

Gettysburg. At dawn on July 2, the battalion marched four miles, arriving very near the battlefield between six and eight in the morning. Colonel E. P. Alexander led one column of the First Corps' guns. General Longstreet had ordered him to keep out of sight of the Federal signal tower on top of Little Round Top. Alexander followed the Chambersburg Road before turning off into open fields, leading to Marsh Creek. His command then followed the course of that stream until they reached a small hill, less than a few hundred yards south of Black Horse Tavern. Colonel Alexander stopped the column there; if they had proceeded over the hill, they would have been spotted by the Yankee signal tower on Little Round Top. The bright young colonel then found a way to advance by easing the guns along the banks of Marsh Creek at a point where it meandered just north of the Curran Farm. There they cut across the meadow south of the hill, heading northeast of the Curran Farm and avoiding Union eyes on Little Round Top. Going only a few hundred yards by this route, the artillery cut back to the road and galloped past the Plank Farm toward the back of Willoughby Run. They then proceeded to a shallow gulley, close to a schoolhouse between the run and a wooded area opposite the Emmitsburg Road. About midday Colonel Alexander rode back to collect the other artillery battalions that had remained with Longstreet's main column.

Often overlooked, during these several days of vigorous marching in June and July heat and humidity and wearing wool uniforms, several hundred men on both sides collapsed with heat stroke and exhaustion, many dying where they fell. Horses also suffered from the heat, collapsing and dying.

General Lee's plan on July 2 called for simultaneous attacks on General Meade's left and right flanks with both infantry and artillery. General Hood of Longstreet's Corps commanded the Confederate right flank, attacking the Federal left. Reilly's Battery anchored the end of the Confederate right flank with a clear and unobstructed view of Little Round Top and Devil's Den and had an excellent position to enfilade the Yankee line for at least a mile and a half. The battery consisted of two twelve-pound Napoleon short range guns, two ten-pound Parrott rifles and two three-inch ordnance rifles for accurate long range firing. Reilly, Ramsay and the Rowan Artillery found themselves in an excellent position to give the Yankees "artillery hell."

General Longstreet, "Lee's war horse," vigorously argued with his commander that he was taking an ill-advised offensive position. Longstreet wanted to redeploy and find a solid defensive position, where he could rely on the strength of interior lines. To accomplish this, he advocated moving around Little Round Top to the right and heading southeast to take up a defensive position at the Pipe Creek Line or somewhere between the Army of the Potomac and Washington. He wanted the Federals to attack the Army of Northern Virginia, and he saw his present situation as Fredericksburg in reverse.

A good many Confederate soldiers did not like fighting on northern soil. They felt that God would not be with them and that the Yankees would fight harder to defend their homeland. Their apprehension had some validity, especially since three of the highest ranking Federal generals, Meade, Hancock and Reynolds, were Pennsylvanians.

Colonel Alexander placed Reilly's Battery to the far right flank of the Confederate line around three thirty in the afternoon of July 2. Hood's and McLaw's divisions gathered in the vicinity of the little schoolhouse, preparing to make their assault on the enemy line, which now extended from Little Round Top to the Peach Orchard. Reilly's battery moved out in front of Hood's division and took a position near the Emmitsburg Road. At once the battery became hotly engaged with a superior Yankee artillery force. General Hunt, who remained in command of the Army of the Potomac's artillery, directed the Federal fire astride his famous pale white horse, "Bill," who was well recognized by the Confederate artillerymen. Typically, and with great effect, he employed powerful, carefully aimed and massive artillery barrages, while most of the Confederate artillery fired rapidly and sporadically at many targets.

Reilly's Battery advanced and crossed the Emmitsburg Road, where they returned Union fire coming from the Peach Orchard and beyond. Colonel Alexander, mounted on his horse "Dixie," saw the overwhelming Federal artillery fire concentrating on Reilly's battery and Hood's division, and sent Cabell's battalion with eighteen guns and another eighteen guns from his own battalion to support them. Reinforced, the Rowan Artillery fired into Union General Daniel Sickles's left flank with great effect. Not to be out-gunned, Hunt called in his artillery reserves, and one of the hottest artillery duels of the war took place on this July afternoon. After Reilly and his fellow Confederate battery commanders "exchanged compliments" with the Yankee artillerists for approximately thirty minutes, General Hood ordered his division to reform and assault Little Round Top, as directed by General Lee.

The Union commanders, seeing the impending attack, rushed troops and artillery to defend their left flank at Little Round Top. During this attack, Reilly's Battery engaged in a sharp artillery duel with guns commanded by Lieutenant Charles E. Hazlett, positioned on top of Little Round Top. Hazlett was killed by a Confederate sharpshooter from Devil's Den and Lieutenant Benjamin F. Rittenhouse took command of the guns as the duel continued. When the Confederate shot and shell struck the granite rocks of Little Round Top, fragments of the granite became like canister, causing great damage to the Union men and their equipment.

After the fight had gone on for about two hours, General Hood was wounded when an artillery fragment hit his left arm, penetrating his biceps, elbow, forearm and hand. Falling from his horse, "Thunder," he was moved to the rear for medical care. The surgeons did not amputate his arm, but for the rest of his life it remained limp and useless. Major Haskell, who shared battalion command with Major Henry in anticipation of Henry's imminent departure, also served as an artillery aide for Hood and accompanied the general when he was wounded. Hood had pleaded with General Longstreet to allow him to encircle Little Round Top on the Union right and attack their rear. Longstreet politely informed Hood that General Lee would not consider this tactic and expected Hood to take the hill from the front. At the time Hood was wounded, his second in command, General Evander McIvor Law of South Carolina, characteristically led the troops on the front line. Before he could be found to take command, night was falling and the battle was winding down.

Reilly's Battery expended over eight hundred and fifty rounds of ammunition in the assault on Little Round Top. Captain Reilly and his "hounds of hell" kept up such a rapid fire that their three-inch rifled Bellona cannon burst. The gunners replaced it with a Union ten-pound Parrott gun, captured by Law's Alabama and Benning's Georgia brigades from Smith's Fourth Independent New York Battery, attached to the Third Corps. During the artillery action on the second day of Gettysburg, the Rowan Artillery opposed a large number of Union batteries, including Smith's, Hazlett's, Winslow's, Bigelow's, Phillips's, Clark's, Hunt's and Ames's. As the battle lines shifted, the North Carolinians possibly engaged several other Union batteries, including Bucklyn's, Thompson's, Seeley's and Turnbull's.

The simultaneous attacks that General Lee had planned for July 2 did not materialize as he wished. Instead, a series of fragmented and uncoordinated Confederate attacks took place at Culp's Hill and Cemetery Ridge, as well as at Little Round Top. These attacks took place hours apart and failed to dislodge the Union defenders. In other areas of the battlefield, the Confederates met with greater success, pushing the Yankees from the Wheatfield, the Peach Orchard, Devil's Den and the Valley of Death.

The limited success of the past two days battles, combined with the overwhelming victories at Fredericksburg and Chancellorsville, encouraged General Lee's confidence in the Army of Northern Virginia. Lee decided to attack the Union center, which he believed was the weakest point in the Federal line, on Friday, July 3. On the night of July 2, General Meade held a council of war with his staff and corps commanders and decided to maintain the Army of the Potomac's defensive position for the anticipated Confederate attack on the next day. These decisions by Generals Lee and Meade resulted in one of the most famous days in the history of American warfare.

After the war, Colonel E. P. Alexander recounted the following event that might have changed the history of the Battle of Gettysburg and the course of the war:

> *It is during the night of July 2nd that General Meade had determined to retreat. This is said to have been testified by his chief of staff, General Butterfield, before the Committee on [the] Conduct of the War. There is also evidence of the existence of a report in the Federal army that a force under Beauregard was approaching to reinforce General Lee. And it is a fact that some weeks, before General Lee had written three letters to President Davis, begging that General Beauregard should be send in person to Culpeper, with even any few old troops which might be scared up out of jails or hospitals just as a source to start rumors from, for he appreciated the insanity of fear for the safety of Washington City. Now Mr. Davis does not seem to have realized the value of this suggestion, for it was surely worth, at least, having Beauregard a few days to it. And Mr. Davis wrote at last a letter to General Lee saying that it was impracticable to get any force under Beauregard. And in his office the immense blunder was made of sending that letter by courier & not putting it in cipher. The courier was captured on July 2 in Greencastle, by Capt. Ulric Dahlgren, who appreciated the importance of this letter, & hurried to Gettysburg with it, reaching there toward midnight & delivering the letter to Meade.*

> *Of all that there is no doubt. And Dahlgren was soon after jumped three grades to rank of colonel, & he is said to have told his friends that his promotion was for capturing a letter & delivering it to General Meade in time to prevent him from retreating from Gettysburg. However this may be it is instructive to note how careless it is to send valuable information around without it in cipher.*

During the Gettysburg campaign, the Army of Northern Virginia hosted several military observers from Europe, including Captain Schreibert of the Prussian Army and, most notably, Lieutenant Colonel Arthur J. L. Fremantle of the

British Coldstream Guards. On the morning of June 30, Fremantle first met the commander of the Army of Northern Viriginia. His description of General Lee provides an excellent image of the beloved Confederate leader.

> *General Lee is almost without exception the handsomest man of his age I ever saw. He is fifty-six years old, tall, broad-shouldered, very well made, well set up — a thorough soldier in appearance; and his manners are most courteous and full of dignity. He is a perfect gentleman in every respect. I imagine no man has so few enemies, or is so universally esteemed. Throughout the South, all agree in pronouncing him to be as near perfection as a man can be. He has none of the vices, such as smoking, drinking, chewing, or swearing and his bitterest enemy never accused him of any of the greater ones. He generally wears a well-worn long gray jacket, a high black felt hat, blue trousers tucked into his Wellington boots.*

> *I never saw him carry arms; and the only mark of his military rank are the three stars on his collar. He rides a handsome horse, which is well groomed. He himself is very neat in his dress and person and in the most arduous marches he always looks smart and clean. His only faults, so far as I can learn, arise from his excessive amiability.*

Another British military commentator, Viscount Wolsely, summed up much international opinion when he wrote of Lee, "He is stamped upon my memory as being apart and superior to all others in every way." The Confederacy and the Army of Northern Virginia expressed great pride in "Marse Robert," and several of his troops commented that they would follow him into hell if necessary.

Fremantle also commented on the Confederate artillery bombardments, "When the cannonade was at its height, a Confederate band of music between the cemetery and ourselves began to play polkas and waltzes, which sounded very curious, accompanied by the hissing and bursting of the shells." He also observed that the Confederate artillerymen in charge of the horses would dig little holes that resembled graves, throwing the earth up at the upper end and then place themselves in these holes when under fire.

On the morning of July 3, 1863, General Lee ordered another unsuccessful attempt to take the Union position, occupying Culp's Hill. A mile east of the town, six thousand Confederate cavalry troops under the command of General Jeb Stuart, engaged in a hot, all day fight to take the Union rear. The five-thousand man Yankee cavalry under General Alfred Pleasonton eventually contained and turned the Confederate cavalry. Both the Union and Confederate horse artillery were hotly engaged in artillery duels, playing a significant part in this cavalry struggle. The Confederate horse artillery consisted of Major James Breathed's battalion, Major William McGregor's battalion, Captain Thomas E. Jackson's battery, Captain William H. Griffin's battery and Captain C. A. Green's Louisiana Guard artillery. They tangled with the First United States Artillery, and Captain Pennington's and Captain Alanson M. Randol's Union batteries. The Confederate batteries held their ground until their ammunition was exhausted and withdrew before dusk.

General Lee ordered General Longstreet's corps to make the assault on the Union center at Cemetery Ridge. The center was defined by a small grouping or clump of trees a little over a mile across an open, undulating field, offering no protection from the Union artillery. Longstreet personally opposed this charge and strongly expressed his certainty that it would fail. He argued in favor of redeploying and taking a defensive position on ground of the southern army's own choosing. Lee insisted on the attack. He believed his troops could break the Union center and give the South a great victory on northern soil, which would help bring the war to an end.

Lee planned to launch a massive artillery cannonade before the assault, paving the way for the Confederate infantry attack by destroying the Union artillery, driving off many Union troops and demoralizing the Federal army. The honor of leading the Confederate infantry charge was given to Major General George E. Pickett of Virginia and Brigadier General James J. Pettigrew of North Carolina. Colonel E. P. Alexander of Longstreet's corps, under the command of Army of Northern Virginia artillery commander William Nelson Pendleton, directed the artillery cannonade.

Colonel Alexander began preparations for the bombardment by placing his First Corps artillery battalions and batteries, totaling seventy-five to eighty guns, in place for the impending cannonade. Reilly's Battery of Henry's battalion remained in position on the far right flank, where it had been since the start of the battle. Colonel Alexander was aware that the Confederate ammunition wagons were not fully loaded when they left the Staunton, Virginia supply depot in June. Now, after expending large amounts of ammunition during the past two days, supplies were even shorter. Alexander estimated that he would only have enough ammunition for a thirty-five to sixty minute cannonade. He also kept in mind that if the charge failed he would need some ammunition left to repulse the advancing "blue bellies."

General Pendleton visited Colonel Alexander to ask if he would have use for nine twelve-pound howitzers from the Third Corps artillery commanded by Colonel R. L. Walker. Colonel Alexander jumped at the offer. He had the very place and use for these short range guns, even though they would not be useful for the long-range cannonade. He immediately rode off with General Pendleton to retrieve them. Colonel Alexander placed Major Charles Richardson, a Virginian from Garnett's Third Corps battalion, in command of the nine howitzers, but did not inform General Pendleton how he planned to use them. He placed them under a cover of foliage known as "the bit of woods" and out of view with fresh men, uninjured horses, and full ammunition chests. According to renowned historian, Ed Bearss, "the bit of woods" is located behind the present-day Virginia monument across Confederate Avenue. Alexander ordered this concealed unit to accompany and follow Pickett's infantry once the charge began. Colonel Alexander also placed Captain M. B. Miller of the Washington Louisiana artillery and his two twelve-pound Napoleons near the Klingel Farm, as signal guns to start the cannonade.

After all the hot and laborious work of placing the First Corps' guns in position, Alexander was begrimed, coatless, and sweat drenched, the symbols of his rank barely visible on the collar of his gray shirt. He limped as a result of a sore knee, bruised when a minie ball passed between his legs the previous day near Little Round Top, tearing his trousers and drawers. Alexander felt as prepared as possible to commence the bombardment of the Federal center. He knew that General Longstreet was looking for every excuse to stop or hold up the charge. However, at one in the afternoon, Longstreet personally gave the order for Captain Miller's signal guns to open fire. One of the Napoleon guns misfired and was quickly made ready and fired. All of Alexander's guns along a two mile line opened on the Yankee center. On the opposite side of the battlefield, General Hunt, the master of mass artillery tactics, returned the fire. Reilly's Battery participated in the largest cannonade that ever occurred on the North American continent. The ground shook and the thunderous noise could be heard for several miles.

After some time had passed, Alexander ordered his caissons back to the ammunition wagons to be refilled. The Yankee artillery was overshooting their target, as were the Confederates. The gunners could not see either in front of or behind them because of the blanket of smoke that covered the battlefield. General Pendleton had moved the ammunition wagons without telling anyone or sending a courier to Alexander to explain where they had been moved. This put a further strain on the southern artillery. The Confederate gunners also had the disadvantage of firing uphill without being able to see their targets, because of the thick gun smoke.

General Hunt's artillery characteristically fired at a slow rate and massed their guns on one target at a time with careful aim. The Union command tried to find a way to fool the Confederates into commencing their infantry attack, while General Hunt conserved enough ammunition for the impending Confederate charge. Hunt also brought up his famous "ghost train" of extra artillery ammunition and supplies, which he had saved for just such an occasion. He then removed eighteen guns from his center to trick the Confederate command into believing that the Union artillery was withdrawing, and encourage the Confederate infantry to begin their charge. These eighteen guns most likely came from Major Thomas W. Osborn's artillery brigade made up of Battery G, Fourth U. S. Artillery; Batteries I and K, First Ohio Artillery; Battery I, First New York Artillery; and the Thirteenth New York Independent Battery.

At 1:35 p.m., Colonel Alexander, seeing the eighteen guns being removed while his own ammunition grew lower by the minute, sent a note to Pickett. It read, "For God's sake come quick. The eighteen guns are gone. Come quick or I can't support you." General Pickett was unaware that Alexander had also been exchanging notes with General Longstreet. Longstreet did not want to take responsibility for ordering the charge and attempted to place the burden on Alexander. Pickett stood before Longstreet and asked him for the order to advance. Longstreet could not say the words. He just nodded his head, lowering his chin to his collar.

During the bombardment, Colonel Alexander had sent Private Arthur Catlett of the Bedford Virginia Light Artillery to bring up Major Richardson and the nine reserve howitzers. Catlett was gone for some time and, when he returned, he informed Alexander that the guns were not where he had left them. "He would not dare to leave there without orders," Alexander barked, "You go again and find him and don't you come back without him." Catlett was gone for a long time. When he finally returned, he informed Alexander that Richardson had certainly disappeared.

After the battle, Alexander learned that General Pendleton had taken four of the howitzers without sending any notice to Alexander. Major Richardson admitted removing the remaining five guns a short distance to avoid the Yankee shells that were exploding all around them as a result of the Union artillery's over-shooting. Colonel Alexander's plan had been for the howitzers to go before the Confederate infantry, blasting holes in the fence line along the Emmitsburg

Road so that the troops could keep up an unrestricted fast pace. Afterwards, the howitzers were to fire into the stone walls protecting the Union defensive line.

General Pickett's Division formed, ready to march across the large open field toward the clump of trees at the Union center. Suddenly, at the far right flank of the Confederate line, Yankee cavalrymen appeared. As soon as he discovered the enemy's presence, General E. M. Law directed his artillery and infantry to the endangered right flank. Reilly's and Bachman's batteries had been firing at the Union center, but Law now ordered them to wheel their guns around and fire into the Federal horsemen. General Law also dispatched his own Georgia infantry brigade to protect the Confederate right flank.

As the Confederates later learned, General Meade had ordered General Alfred Pleasonton to launch the cavalry charge against the Confederate right flank. Pleasonton, in turn, ordered General Hugh Judson Kilpatrick's two brigades to begin the attack. Mounted on his horse, "Old Spot," Kilpatrick ordered General Elon J. Farnsworth to lead the charge. Farnsworth protested against the futility of this move. Kilpatrick questioned his bravery and dared him to lead the charge, adding, "Then, by God, if you are afraid to go, I will lead the charge myself." Farnsworth reluctantly complied and was killed when the Confederate forces drove his brigade back, inflicting significant losses.

While Reilly's Battery was engaged in repelling Farnsworth's ill-fated flank attack, the cannonade ceased and more than twelve thousand Confederate soldiers marched from Seminary Ridge in parade dress formation to launch the heroic attack against the Union center, known to history as "Pickett's-Pettigrew's Charge." The Federal forces watched in utter amazement and awe. They could not help but to admire the intense patriotism and desperate dedication of these men. Once they came within range, the Union artillery opened up on them with shot and shell, mowing the columns of Confederates down like blades of grass. Still they kept coming, dressing their lines down to keep the advance in good order.

The Union batteries poured fire from all points along the line. Hazlett's Battery on Little Round Top, with its six ten-pound Parrott rifles, fired directly into the Confederate right flank with devastating effect. When the Confederates approached within four hundred yards, the Union gunners switched to using deadly canisters and double canisters, blasting great holes in the southern line. The result can only be compared to a slaughterhouse. The remnants of the attacking lines converged on the Union center with officers falling and formations melting away in the confusion. Major General Winfield Scott Hancock, commanding the

Union Second Corps, which held the center, fell wounded. His men, remembering the similar carnage they had endured at Marye's Heights, took their revenge and shouted, "Fredericksburg!" as they fired. Lieutenant Alonzo H. Cushing's Federal battery inflicted great losses before Cushing was killed by a bullet to his mouth as he shouted for his guns to fire.

As General Hunt neared the center of the Confederate attack, he reined in his horse Bill, near the clump of trees and discharged his pistol into the charging Confederates. Suddenly, no less than five minie balls hit Bill. The horse staggered, then collapsed, pinning General Hunt firmly to the ground. Hunt tried desperately to free himself, realizing that the swarm of advancing Confederates could easily kill or capture him. Finally, a group of Federal gunners managed to free Hunt. After this incident, General Hunt later recalled, "The display of secesh battle flags was splendid and scary." Over ten Confederate battle flags were captured. After fifteen minutes inside the Union lines, the Confederates straggled back to their lines, General Longstreet and Colonel Alexander prepared for a Union counterattack that never came.

General Lee, the personification of reassuring calm and dependability, met the beaten remnants of the charge and gave them his heartfelt words, saying over and over that this disaster was all his fault. Over five thousand six hundred men, nearly fifty percent of the Confederates who made the charge, became casualties, compared to approximately one thousand five hundred Union troops. Colonel E. P. Alexander expressed the following thoughts on Gettysburg:

> I think it a reasonable estimate to say that sixty per cent of our chances for a great victory were lost by our continuing the aggressive. And we may easily imagine the boon it was to General Meade...to be relieved from the burden of making any difficult decision, such as he would have had to do if Lee had been satisfied with his victory of the first day; & then taken a strong position & stood on defensive. Now the gods had flung to Meade more than impudence itself could have dared to pray for — a position unique among all the battlefields of the war, certainly adding fifty per cent to his already superior force, and an adversary stimulated by success to an utter disregard of all physical disadvantages & ready to face for nearly three quarters of a mile the very worst that all his artillery & infantry could do.

The artillery losses for the Battle of Gettysburg included ninety-four Confederates killed, four hundred and thirty-eight wounded, and seventy-eight missing for a total of six hundred and ten. Reilly's Battery suffered two men killed and six wounded, as well as three horses killed and four wounded. Union artillery losses from killed, wounded and missing numbered more than seven hundred. Cushing's Battery suffered the heaviest loss of all batteries engaged, as a result of the desperate hand-to-hand fighting at the stone wall. Troops involved in the Battle of Gettysburg totaled one hundred and seventy thousand-- ninety-five thousand from the Army of the Potomac and seventy-five thousand from the Army of Northern Virginia.

Military experts and historians have debated and analyzed the reasons for the Confederate defeat at Gettysburg ever since the battle took place. Many have cited the loss of General Stonewall Jackson at Chancellorsville as a prime factor, arguing that Jackson's sheer presence and aggressive behavior would have had a great psychological effect. Some have speculated that Jackson would have advocated "raising the black flag" and fighting until one army or the other was completely destroyed, but these conjectures only open a Pandora 's box of "what if."

The Union had a far superior chief of artillery in General Henry J. Hunt, a fact which was demonstrated time and again on many battlefields. The Confederate chief of artillery, General William N. Pendleton, was a well-meaning but incompetent artillery officer, who essentially served as a liaison between General Lee and the corps artillery commanders. His failure to properly evaluate the ground for Pickett's-Pettigrew's Charge, poor artillery organization, and lack of coordination between artillery corps commanders, as well as a confused overall artillery command structure, lack of reserve artillery and misconceptions over the availability of ammunition, all contributed to the southern artillery failure at Gettysburg. General Pendleton simply lacked the artillery knowledge, experience and skills of General Hunt.

The old artillery fox, Hunt, also had at his disposal his famous "ghost train" of extra ammunition that he kept a secret from his commanding officers, men, and quartermasters. Hunt hid this train with his reserve artillery. It contained enough ammunition and supplies to give each cannon in the Army of the Potomac an extra twenty rounds of ammunition.

Differences in equipment and technology also gave the Union artillery a distinct advantage. Confederate artillery fuses were often defective and as many as eighty percent of the shells and case shot exploded too soon or not at all. The Confederates analyzed this problem to no avail. They could not understand why captured Union fuses and ordnance worked so well in their guns, while their own failed. After the war the secret was exposed.

Lammont DuPont of the famous gunpowder manufacturing company had discovered that adding graphite to the gunpowder during a twelve-hour tumbling process dramatically reduced the absorption of moisture from the atmosphere, giving the powder a longer storage life and far more efficiency in its use with fuses. Without this technology, Confederate gunpowder and fuses faced a great disadvantage. It required the high temperature of a cap or friction primer to ignite Confederate gunpowder. Because of the absorption of atmospheric moisture, cannon tube gases were not hot enough to fully ignite the powder in the fuses. This presented a major technological advantage for the Union artillery, an advantage so evident that General Hunt made several observations on the amount of defective Confederate shells. At Gettysburg, Hunt also made efficient use of his knowledge that the Union artillery had more rifled guns for long-range firing.

The Union lines of communication were also far superior at Gettysburg. The signal station at the heights of Little Round Top provided a commanding view of the battlefield for miles. The Federals also strung telegraph wire in trees along their entire line, providing the high command with excellent intelligence on troop movements at very short notice.

The Army of the Potomac also had the advantage of an operational system of railroads. Brigadier General Herman Haupt earned the nickname of "Lincoln's railroad man." Born March 26, 1817, Haupt became the youngest man ever to graduate from West Point, completing his studies at the age of eighteen. His finest hour came at Gettysburg, where he created and arranged a Union rail system that could deliver one thousand five hundred tons of supplies per day and evacuate over sixteen thousand wounded soldiers.

In addition to these impressive Union advantages, the Confederate high command suffered from a lack of staff officers to prepare written orders. The absence of written orders hampered the Army of Northern Virginia throughout the war, but was especially critical at Gettysburg. Oral orders delivered by couriers or given at command meetings sometimes led to misinterpretations of what the high command expected or requested. At Gettysburg this deficiency caused much confusion and delay in Confederate troop movements and attacks.

The absence of General Jeb Stuart's cavalry, which attempted to encircle the Army of the Potomac and raid the rich Pennsylvania farmlands, left the Army of Northern Virginia without its "eyes and ears." Having to move blindly through enemy territory with very little knowledge of the Union army's whereabouts, strengths, and numbers created a great disadvantage for General Lee and the Army of Northern Virginia.

After the Battle of Gettysburg, the South realized that it had reached the breaking point of its resources. General Lee could never again take the offensive. Aside from small raids into "Yankee Land," the Army of Northern Virginia would be compelled to fight a defensive war, expending men, ammunition and supplies in an ongoing effort to protect Richmond. Colonel Arthur Fremantle is quoted with saying at Gettysburg, "Isn't this splendid, I wouldn't have missed it for the world." But the impressive, bloody battle turned out to be anything but splendid for Lee's army.

After the Pickett-Pettigrew Charge on July 3, 1863, Reilly's Battery remained at their original post on the Confederate far right flank. They changed position the following day, but remained on the battlefield until six in the evening, when they took up a line of march which lasted throughout the night in very heavy rains. They kept up the march until two in the afternoon of July 5, when they encamped at South Mountain. The next day they marched an additional sixteen miles to a point near Hagerstown, Maryland, where they remained until July 10. On the morning of the tenth, they left camp and assumed a defensive position on the right of the Confederate artillery line in the vicinity of Downsville, Maryland.

General Lee and his engineers, including Colonel E. P. Alexander and Major Jedediah Hotchkiss, the excellent topographical engineer who had served Stonewall Jackson so well in the Valley Campaign, laid out an excellent defensive line to protect the Army of Northern Virginia's crossing of the Potomac River from a possible attack by the Army of the Potomac. The river was very high as a result of the past several days' heavy rains. This defensive line protected the Confederate army over an area between Williamsport, Maryland and Hagerstown and Downsville. Colonel Alexander's excellent gun emplacements gave the battery gunners a perfect field of fire should the enemy decide to launch an attack. Major James Dearing's battalion and Colonel Cabell's battalion held the positions to the left of Reilly's Battery.

The Rowan Artillery remained in this position through July 11 and 12, a few days of relaxation, which the men savored mainly because of the great abundance of ripe wild cherries and raspberries. Nearby farms also provided potatoes, vegetables and fattened chickens for the camp's cooking pot. Lawrence Ward, a Negro from Plymouth, North Carolina, served as the battery's cook until October 31, 1864. At eight in the evening on July 13, the battery was back on the road to the Potomac River. July 14 found the Rowan Artillery crossing the Potomac at Falling Waters on a newly build Confederate pontoon bridge and marching eight miles to Martinsburg, Virginia. The men of Reilly's Battery were greatly relieved to return to Confederate soil without incident.

CHAPTER VII

EBB TIDE OF THE CONFEDERACY

By July 24, 1863, the Rowan Artillery had marched over eighty-five miles, arriving and encamping near Culpeper Court House, where they remained until August 1. Captain Reilly received word on July 31 that command of Major Henry's Battalion had passed to Major Haskell. As a veteran artillerist of many years, Reilly was not willing to be subject to the command of a twenty-two year old, who had no military background and whose battlefield experience was confined to one day at Gaines' Mill, several days in North Carolina and two days at Gettysburg.

Discouraged and angered, Reilly addressed letters of resignation to both the authorities of North Carolina and the Confederate government in Richmond. His resignation was not accepted, but it brought the results he had long sought. Backed up by letters from General Law and the intervention of leading citizens of Salisbury, North Carolina, including F. E. Sholer, Reilly was promoted to the rank of major of the Tenth Regiment of North Carolina Troops by Governor Vance on September 7. The official promotion papers did not reach Reilly in Virginia until October 23. The next day Reilly passed the battery command on to Captain John Ramsay and the Rowan Artillery became known as Ramsay's Battery. Both men were elated to finally receive their promotions, as were other men in the battery who now moved up the ladder of rank.

As fate would have it, on October 27 Reilly received a commission from President Davis, appointing him to the rank of major in the Confederate service. After waiting so long for this recognition, he returned it with regret, explaining that he had already accepted a commission from the State of North Carolina. Reilly remained with the Army of Northern Virginia until the spring of 1864, serving in a variety of artillery positions, including service as second in command of Haskell's Battalion.

On April 22, 1864, the Adjutant and Inspector General of the Confederate States issued Special Order Number 94/4, ordering Reilly to report to the Department of North Carolina and Southern Virginia under the command of General P. G. T. Beauregard at Weldon, North Carolina. On May 1, Special Order Number 2 ordered Major Reilly to report to General W. H. C. Whiting at the mouth of the Cape Fear River in Wilmington, North Carolina. With great pleasure Major Reilly reported to duty under the command of his old friend, Whiting, and remained there until the end of the war. Reilly especially appreciated this assignment since it brought him home to Wilmington to his wife and four children, whom he had not seen since 1862.

According to Confederate official records and company muster rolls, Reilly was furloughed for twenty-one days early in 1862. He most likely returned home to Wilmington to attend to his wife and family. Records of the Confederate Medical Director's Office in Richmond indicate that he was admitted to Hospital Number 10 on October 13, 1862 and then furloughed again for sixty days. No records survive to determine the nature of his illness, but he was able to return to duty in December just before the Battle of Fredericksburg.

The Rowan Artillery, now Ramsay's Battery, did not accompany General Longstreet, Colonel Alexander and Hood's Texas Brigade when they transferred west and fought at Chickamauga on September 18 through September 20, and in east Tennessee during the winter of 1863-1864. Although the two organizations were never closely associated after the Gettysburg Campaign, the Texans, who remained with Hood, never forgot the men of the Rowan Artillery. When they formed a veterans association in the early 1870s, they invited the battery to join them and participate in their annual reunions.

On October 27, 1863, near Brandy Station, Virginia, Captain Ramsay received a new battle flag for the battery. This flag was most likely a Richmond Depot third bunting issue, a thirty-six inch by thirty-six inch artillery wool battle flag. With the departure of Longstreet's corps, Ramsay's Battery joined General A. P. Hill's Third Corps, under the direct command of Hill's chief of artillery, General Rubin L. Walker. Walker, a native of Logan, Virginia, graduated from the Virginia Military Institute in 1845 and worked as a civil engineer. Southern ladies considered General R. L. Walker one of the best looking officers in the Army of Northern Virginia.

After Gettysburg, President Lincoln strongly criticized General Meade for failing to pursue General Lee aggressively and allowing him to cross the Potomac and concentrated his army behind the Rapidan River in Orange County,

Virginia. Meade's delayed pursuit resulted in the running five battles of the Bristoe Campaign from October 13 to November 7, 1863, actually a series of artillery duels and maneuvers. Lee attempted to turn Meade's right flank, forcing Meade, despite his superior numbers, to withdraw to the line of the Orange and Alexandria Railroad. Detaching troops to the fronts in Georgia and Tennessee weakened both armies. The Rowan Artillery made a very good showing during the Bristoe Campaign.

The Bristoe Campaign was followed by the equally inconclusive Mine Run Campaign from November 27 to December 2, 1863. Mine Run consisted of a series of battles as both armies tried to out-maneuver each other. The Army of Northern Virginia's flanking movements were characterized by uncoordinated attacks and numerous miscommunications, leading General Lee to comment, "I am too old to command this army. We should never have permitted those people to get away." The Rowan Artillery, as part of Haskell's battalion, took part in this maneuvering with A. P. Hill's Third Corps.

The Rowan Artillery and the rest of Haskell's battalion began their winter encampment near Cobham's Depot in Albemarle County, Virginia, located on the Orange and Alexandria Railroad between Charlottesville and Gordonsville. They stayed there throughout the winter of 1863-1864, resting, drilling and trying to recruit new artillery troops. On Friday, April 22, 1864, General Longstreet and newly promoted Brigadier General E. P. Alexander returned to the Army of Northern Virginia. General Lee honored the return of his First Corps with a grand review, the last such parade he would ever hold for the Army of Northern Virginia. Mounted on his noble horse, Traveller, General Lee rode at the head of his staff. They positioned themselves upon a high knoll. When the artillery bugles sounded, the battalions, including Ramsay's Battery, thundered out a loud salute. The general acknowledged the artillery by taking off his hat and baring his gray head. Lee and his staff then rode by to inspect the artillery. The men shouted, cried and waved their battle flags. They regarded General Lee as their brave and gallant commander, the personification of southern manhood and a true man of God. Each soldier seemed to have a special bond and sentiment with his general.

On May 4, 1864, Ramsay's Battery received orders to advance. They marched through Orange Court House and on to Richard's Store along the Orange Plank Road east of Locust Grove, then to an area known as the Wilderness.

The Wilderness was true to its name, encompassing a little over seventy square miles in Spotsylvania County, Virginia. A massive tangle of underbrush, forest, scrub and very rough terrain made this region of central Virginia almost impenetrable.

By March 1864 President Lincoln had promoted Ulysses S. Grant to the newly created rank of lieutenant general and appointed him general-in-chief of all the Union armies. Grant, from Georgetown, Ohio, had entered West Point at the age of seventeen and graduated in 1843, twenty-first out of a class of thirty-nine. He was noted for his heavy drinking, but he won battles and pursued the enemy with bulldog determination. Lincoln reportedly said of Grant, "Find out what he drinks so I can give it to the rest of my generals."

Lincoln and Grant created a master plan for an all-out attack to destroy the Confederacy. While Grant launched the Army of the Potomac on the Overland Campaign to capture Richmond, General William Tecumseh Sherman, with sixty-eight thousand men and sixty-five guns advanced against General Joe Johnston and his Army of Tennessee in northern Georgia. This tactic allowed the Union to keep unrelenting pressure on the Confederacy with a coordinated two-front war. Grant also stopped the prisoner exchange program to put more pressure on the Confederate war effort, reasoning that the North could afford the loss of manpower while the South could not.

The Overland Campaign actually involved four separate Union armies. Grant, with the Second, Fifth, Sixth and Ninth Corps, crossed the Rapidan with a force of one hundred and forty-four thousand men. His artillery, commanded by General Henry J. Hunt, consisted of two hundred and seventy-four guns plus a siege train, containing one hundred and six heavy guns and six one-hundred-pound rifles. Hunt intended to use these heavy guns to pound the city of Richmond into submission. The approximately sixteen thousand men of the Union cavalry were all armed with new, breechloading carbines that gave them double the fire power of the Confederate cavalry with its muzzleloaders.

Major General Franz Sigel, a German immigrant who commanded the Department of West Virginia, was to move up the Shenandoah Valley to Staunton, pronounced Stanton by locals. His army consisted of fifteen thousand men and forty guns.

Brigadier General George Crook of Ohio, commanding the Second Division of the Department of West Virginia, was to move on Staunton, using the Virginia Central Railroad by way of Lewisburg. At Staunton, Crook planned to unite with Sigel and advance on Richmond from the west. General Crook's force contained nine thousand men and twenty-four guns.

Major General Benjamin F. Butler of Massachusetts organized the Army of the James at Fortress Monroe, located at the tip of the Peninsula opposite Norfolk. He was to move on Richmond from the east along the south side of the James River. The Army of the James included a large fleet of gunboats, ferry boats and other types of river craft, plus two corps of infantry, the Tenth and the eighteenth, numbering thirty-seven thousand three hundred and seventy men. Butler's artillery consisted of eighty-eight guns and his cavalry contained five thousand mounted men.

Together, these armies gave General Grant an overwhelming force of two hundred twenty-seven thousand men and five hundred eighty-two guns, contrasted with General Lee's ninety-two thousand men and three hundred guns. The numbers spoke for themselves, foreshadowing the eventual outcome of the war. In addition, the Anaconda Plan was wrapping its coils tighter and tighter, as the Union navy enlarged its blockading fleet. Despite these odds, the determined men of the Army of Northern Virginia, led by General Lee, remained dedicated to the cause.

At the Wilderness on May 4, 1864, General Lee awaited the arrival of Lieutenant General Longstreet and his First Corps, which he had posted twenty-five miles west to protect the crucial railroad junction at Gordonsville. Lee decided to put his Second and Third Corps into action in an effort to engage Grant before he moved south toward Richmond. The two corps initiated a successful attack before nightfall brought an end to the fighting.

On the morning of May 5, Union General Hancock with forty thousand men resumed the fighting by attacking General A. P. Hill's Third Corps. Lee was unable to send reinforcements from General Ewell's Second Corps, because Ewell also came under a heavy Union attack. Outnumbered and losing ground, General Lee desperately looked for the arrival of Longstreet's First Corps. At noon, just when he was needed most, Longstreet arrived to hurl his corps at Hancock, whose men had become tired and disorganized. Reeling from Longstreet's attack, Hancock retreated to the Brock Road, but Longstreet did not have sufficient troops to continue the attack and complete his victory.

As General Longstreet and his staff rode back to their lines, Confederate troops commanded by General William Mahone mistook the mounted men through the thick underbrush for Yankees. They were wearing new uniforms made of "Richmond gray," a gray so dark it was almost black. Mahone's men fired a volley into the horsemen, wounding some and hitting General Longstreet in the neck and knocking him off his horse. Longstreet was rushed to a hospital tent, where surgeons discovered that the bullet had entered his throat and exited the back of his neck. It cut nerves that controlled the movement of his right arm. Lucky to survive a wound of this severity, Longstreet did not return to duty until October 19, 1864. General Richard H. Anderson of Charleston, South Carolina, an 1842 graduate of West Point, took temporary command of the First Corps until Longstreet's return.

General Alexander arrived late in the morning of May 6 with the First Corps artillery, including Haskell's Battalion and Ramsay's Battery. General Lee soon ordered him to send the First Corps artillery back to Parker's Store, because of the impossibility of using the guns in the thick woods where the infantry fighting took place. Alexander rode back and collected his artillery, placing them at Parker's Store, where they remained inactive throughout the Battle of the Wilderness. Lee's army emerged victorious in the Battle of the Wilderness, where the infantry fought hand-to-hand and blood flowed freely in the tangled underbrush.

After the terrible beating Lee had inflicted on Grant in the Wilderness, many observers, Union and Confederate alike, expected Grant to retreat across the Rapidan River, "lick his wounds" and rest, as other Union commanders had done. Grant had other plans. Despite his heavy casualties, he realized that for the Army of Northern Virginia's tens of thousands, he had hundreds of thousands at his disposal. A war of attrition became Grant's main strategy to subdue and conquer the Confederates.

In an effort to outflank the Confederates, General Grant rushed to the southeast, trying to get between the Army of Northern Virginia and Richmond. General Lee sent Jeb Stuart and his cavalry to block Grant's move and hold the Union army back until the Confederate infantry could come up in support. On the morning of May 8, between three and ten o'clock, Haskell's Battalion camped near the Zion Church until a courier arrived with orders to move quickly to aid Stuart at Spotsylvania.

During most of the day, the battalion moved from the direction of Spotsylvania Court House, taking a position pointing up the Brock Road. From six to eleven that evening, they continued to move up the Brock Road to a position near the intersection of that road and the Old Court House Road near the Block House. Here they soon hotly engaged the enemy. On May 9, Haskell's battalion advanced to a new position in a field near the Perry and Durrett houses, just off the Old Court House Road, where they stayed until May 14.

Haskell was able to set up the Rowan Artillery and his other batteries in echelon and far enough apart to protect each other from Union infantry attacks with a devastating crossfire. At one time the guns were firing in three different directions as the Union infantry advanced on them. In addition to this engagement, Haskell was ordered to take two unnamed batteries to the center of fighting at a curve in the lines known as the Bloody Angle or the Mule Shoe. Here Major Watson's Second Corps artillery guns had been partially disabled. A courier stopped Haskell before he arrived to reinforce Watson, because the Confederates had already beaten back the enemy attack.

On the morning of May 14, Haskell's battalion moved just past the Zion Church. They remained there until May 19, when they moved south with the rest of the First Corps to block Grant's continuing flanking movements. From May 23 to May 26, 1864, Ramsay's Battery participated in a number of small actions, known collectively as the Battle of North Anna.

During one of these engagements on the south side of the North Anna River at Hanover Junction on May 25, Private Farley Eller, number one man with the rammer, and Private Turner Billups, number three man attending the vent, were badly wounded by the premature discharge of their cannon. Private Eller lost two of his fingers and a splinter of the sponge staff entered his arm. Private Billups badly burned his left thumb, which was amputated not long after the incident. Private Eller retired as an invalid and received his parole at Salisbury, North Carolina on May 11, 1865. Private Billups returned to service and was captured at Amelia Court House on April 5, 1865. Taken to the infamous Yankee prison at Point Lookout, Maryland, he took the oath of allegiance on June 23, 1865.

Undeterred by the carnage at Spotsylvania or by Lee's defensive maneuvering, Grant continued moving around the Confederate right flank to the south and the east. As a result, three small engagements occurred at Haw's Shop, Totopotomoy, and Old Church. Experienced troops comprised Grant's heaviest losses during the Overland Campaign. He replaced them with raw recruits and unseasoned troops taken from the defenses around Washington, D.C.

Desperately recalling dispersed troops from outlying forts, Lee succeeded in replacing almost all of the twenty thousand men lost blocking Grant's Overland Campaign. By June 1, these veteran Confederates had entrenched themselves in a very strong position at Cold Harbor, Virginia, named for a local tavern that served cold food. The Confederate lines now ran seven miles from north to south.

Ammunition as well as troops were in increasingly short supply, calling for innovative thinking on the part of Confederate commanders. On May 10, 1864, General William Nelson Pendleton wrote to Lieutenant Colonel Briscoe G. Baldwin, chief of ordnance for the Army of Northern Virginia. He inquired about procuring stink shells that could be fired by howitzers into the Federal lines.

These shells would deliver offensive gases, making it intolerable for the Yankees to hold their position. He also requested hand grenades to support Confederate infantry when they attacked Federal breastworks. Lieutenant Colonel Baldwin replied that he had no stink shells on hand, but could make them if ordered. He had one thousand hand grenades of the U.S. pattern in stock, as well as Rains's designed tubes, which gave them superior exploding capabilities. With the materials available, he could make another one thousand. By this stage of the war, growing material shortages seriously limited the Confederate ability to produce sufficient ammunition.

On June 2, Haskell's battalion moved into position with General Pickett's division, most likely on the northern part of the Confederate line. The battalion enfiladed the advancing enemy line, inflicting heavy casualties on the Union troops. The following day, Haskell's command helped to repel a massive Union assault on the Confederate lines. They began firing at long range, but the Yankees eventually advanced to within three hundred yards of their guns, partially protected by Union artillery counterfire. Haskell continued his devastating artillery barrage on advancing Federal infantry, creating slaughter all along the battle line. Wave after wave of Union troops charged to certain death before the Confederate trenches. This type of defense used by the Confederates laid the foundation for a new type of strategy, trench warfare.

Grant's army suffered tremendous losses, his Overland Campaign costing the Union sixty-five thousand men killed and wounded. Undeterred, Grant kept advancing, earning him the nickname, "The Butcher." The Army of Northern Virginia frantically tried to stop Grant's flanking movements, but the overwhelming Union force proved unstoppable. On June 14, Grant crossed the James River at Wyanoke Neck with the town of Petersburg as his objective. Five railroads converged at Petersburg. The Petersburg and Weldon, Norfolk and Petersburg, and the Petersburg and City Point lines linked the city to southern seaports, while the Southside Railroad from Lynchburg brought supplies from the interior. Except for the Richmond and Danville Railroad, the Richmond and Petersburg Railroad provided the only rail service reaching the Confederate capital.

On June 15, after three days of continuous fighting, the Federals captured the Confederate defensive position just east of Petersburg. Lee's army arrived just in time to block this Federal assault and establish a shorter defensive line closer to the city. The Army of Northern Virginia began to prepare its siege defense and fortifications along a line over twenty-two miles long, from east of Richmond to south of Petersburg. This proved to be the Army of Northern

Virginia's last line of defense in their desperate effort to save the Confederate capital from capture. For two hundred and ninety-two heart-breaking days, the Confederate troops endured starvation and lack of sleep, reduced to wearing rags in the trenches of Petersburg.

Captain Ramsay's medical records reveal that he was sick from April 20 to May 1, and did not take part in the Overland Campaign. Confederate official records and company muster rolls indicate that on April 20, 1864, he was diagnosed with "febris typhordes" at General Hospital Number 4 in Richmond. This disease, very common in the army, resulted from consuming contaminated food, such as raw vegetables or water containing the typhi bacteria. Those with "febris typhordes" who did not die, usually manifested symptoms for life, including stomach pain, headache, fever, diarrhea, and a slow heart rate. The condition could disappear for months, then suddenly reappear. Treatment during the 1860s consisted of bed rest, mercury pills, diaphoretics, bleeding, opium, cathartics or mild purgatives.

On May 9, Ramsay obtained thirty days' sick leave to return home to Salisbury. This time he was diagnosed with "periostitis," meaning inflammation of the connective tissue of most bones except the joints, similar to a bad case of rheumatism. Doctors during this period treated "periostitis" with baths and doses of quinine mixed with alcohol and laudanum. By June 1864, Ramsay returned to his battery. They were in position at the siege lines in front of Petersburg.

During the war many Confederate soldiers used their own home remedies for numerous types of illness. One of the most unusual was General E. P. Alexander's cure for dysentery, a mixture of chloroform, brandy, peppermint and laudanum. Alexander claimed this concoction served its purpose.

Lack of fresh fruits and vegetables in the troops' diet contributed to many diseases. Occasionally soldiers could obtain dried fruits, primarily apples, and from time to time citrus. Canned foods, principally oysters and certain types of meat, were available on a limited basis, but were often not very palatable. The soldiers also consumed pickled eggs and vegetables along with salted meats, when available. Sauerkraut served as an effective supplement to the troops' staple diet of hardtack and pork fat. The Confederates preferred to drink tea, but tea leaves were hard to keep and transport. Coffee beans, when available, stayed fresher and were far easier to carry. Thus, coffee became an increasingly popular drink. Because they lacked coffee grinders, soldiers often used the butts of their rifles to break up the coffee beans.

In June 1864, General E. P. Alexander kept very busy overseeing the placement of the First Corps guns, mainly on the north side of the James River. He was particularly concerned with a weak area at Petersburg, called Elliott's Salient, because it was located only four hundred feet from the Federal lines. Located near the Blandford Church and Cemetery Hill, Elliott's Salient was a well fortified Confederate position, but Alexander sensed some Yankee mischief and worried about the amount of Confederate artillery protecting the salient. On June 20, he placed six iron Coehorn mortars in the ravines behind Elliott's Salient. A Confederate Coehorn mortar weighed three hundred pounds and was fitted with special handles, which made it easier to move. It took four men to carry it into firing position.

Alexander then moved Haskell's sixteen-gun battalion, including Ramsay's Battery, to the Sunken Jerusalem Road, six hundred yards to the rear of the salient. He placed Lieutenant Colonel Haskell in command of all the guns and mortars, ordering him not to break ground or expose the battalion, and to keep the guns completely concealed from the Yankees. Alexander's foresight and intuition proved to be a blessing. General Alexander strongly believed that the "blue bellies" were digging a tunnel and pushed General Lee to dig counter-tunnels to uncover the plan.

On Wednesday, June 30, while inspecting the Federal position at Elliott's Salient, Alexander was wounded in the left shoulder by a Union sharpshooter. Although not fatal, this wound put Alexander out of action for several weeks. Surgeons removed the bullet and sent the general home to Fairfield Plantation in Washington, Georgia to recuperate under the care of his wife, Betty, known as "Miss Teen," and his family. During Alexander's absence, Colonel Frank Huger served as acting chief of artillery of the First Corps. A South Carolinian, Huger graduated from West Point in the Class of 1860. While at the Military Academy, he and Alexander became friends.

General Alexander's suspicions were realized at four-forty in the morning of July 30, when the Federal mine exploded. Lieutenant Colonel Henry Pleasants, commanding the Forty-Eighth Pennsylvania and a mining engineer by profession, and his men had dug a tunnel five hundred and eighty-five feet long under the Confederate line at Elliott's Salient. The Federals then blew the salient out of existence with eight thousand pounds of gunpowder. The explosion blasted a crater roughly two hundred feet long, eighty feet wide, and thirty feet deep. It demolished the Eighteenth South Carolina regiment, Pegram's battery, and over half of the Twenty-Third South Carolina along with all their supplies and equipment, sending them and the earth itself flying through the air for hundreds of yards. The sound of the blast sent men and horses running in all directions in utter confusion.

The Crater explosion was followed by a Federal attack, commanded by General James F. Ledlie of the Ninth Corps' First Division, along with two other divisions and four thousand three hundred Negro troops. When the Federal troops arrived at the crest of the Crater, they were dumbstruck and paused to gaze at the great hole. This caused the brigades to stop short and become inextricably mixed up. The commanders frantically yelled for their troops to move forward and, when they did, they jumped, fell, tumbled, and slid into the hole filled with debris and dead and dying men. Union reinforcements then poured into and around the Crater until by eight-thirty that morning fifteen thousand confused Yankees filled the area in and around the Crater.

When the surrounding Confederates heard the explosion, they scrambled to plug the breach in their line. Colonel Haskell, Captain Ramsay, and their guns were prepared. Following orders from First Corps headquarters, Haskell had kept his battalion's horses harnessed and ready. The men slept by their guns and Haskell slept in his tent fully clothed, his horse saddled. When he heard the horrific explosion, he ordered his orderly-bugler to call the batteries to order. The artillerymen dashed to the hill, took a position on the plank road in front of the Crater, and began firing their guns and the iron Coehorn mortars, which they had brought from the ravine behind Elliott's Salient. The battalion's fire on the disorganized Yankees stopped them from pouring through the breach and charging on to Petersburg.

The Federal confusion and the southern artillery's quick response gave Confederate commanders valuable time to rush troops in to plug the breach and drive the Yankees back with extremely heavy losses. Before they were supported by Confederate infantry, the Rowan Artillery and the rest of Haskell's Battalion stopped the enemy advance. Major General William Mahone's infantry then pushed the Federals back with courageous point-blank firing and hand-to-hand combat, using bayonets and rifle butts. On the Union side, the Negro troops that spearheaded the final attack bore the brunt of this brutal fighting.

Several accounts of the fighting in the Crater tell of moments when a former slave in the Union army and his Confederate master met again on the battlefield. A few descriptions of the aftermath of the battle recount instances where a Negro soldier, lying wounded, asked his one-time master for help. The former masters brought water to the wounded men and did all in their power to make them as comfortable as possible.

The Battle of the Crater proved a costly and miserable failure for the Union. The Army of the Potomac lost four thousand killed, captured, or wounded. The Army of Northern Virginia lost one thousand five hundred.

As the Siege of Petersburg continued, the men of both armies settled into the grueling routine of trench warfare, occasionally punctuated by active combat. General Alexander returned to duty on August 15, 1864. His friend, Lieutenant Colonel Haskell, informed him how his foresight helped save the Army of Northern Virginia from certain disaster at the Crater.

For a short time in August 1864, Ramsay left the Rowan Artillery under the command of Lieutenant Ezekiel Myers of Salisbury, North Carolina. During his absence his horse died from one of the many diseases that plagued animals in the Confederate service.

Fort Harrison, a salient on the Confederate Petersburg line, held a commanding position overlooking the James River. Located about one mile from Chaffin's Bluff and seven miles from Richmond, it was an important part of the Confederate defense. Union troops captured Fort Harrison on September 29, 1864. The next day the Confederates made a desperate, but ultimately unsuccessful, effort to retake this fort.

Ramsay's Battery, as part of Haskell's Battalion, joined General Charles William Field's Division on October 1 and crossed the James River from the Petersburg side in another attempt to recapture Fort Harrison. On October 7, during one of several failed efforts known as the Battle of Darbytown Road, Lieutenant Colonel Haskell narrowly escaped death. Haskell began the battle mounted on a tall, handsome horse, its head looking more like a deer. When his battery opened fire, he sent his horse to the rear and mounted a small battery horse. During the ensuing fight, a musketball split his scalp to the bone, leaving a six-inch gash on top of his head. If he had been riding the taller horse, the ball might have hit him between the eyes, killing him instantly.

General Lee, realizing that he was unable to withstand the loss of men that the Union continued to inflict, constantly struggled to replenish his army. On October 8, he wrote to Governor Zebulon Vance of North Carolina at Raleigh and to General William H. C. Whiting at Wilmington, requesting troops. Lee specifically mentioned Major Reilly, complimenting him and remarking that he would like the major to command an infantry unit or an artillery battalion in the Army of Northern Virginia. Reilly's transfer never materialized.

On October 19, General Longstreet returned to duty, recovered from the wounds he had received at the Wilderness. The officers and men of the First

Corps welcomed him warmly, and his presence brought a momentary lift in their spirits. Within months, however, General Grant's war of attrition took an increasingly irreparable toll.

Ramsay's Battery often split into sections of guns and moved to various locations where needed to ward off Federal attacks. They encountered the enemy at the Howlett Line and General Pickett's Line north of the James, although few full-scale engagements developed. Lee's flanks were becoming so thinly stretched that his line could not be defended.

Chapter VIII

Federals Attack the Gibraltar of the South

Major James Reilly assumed his duties at Fort Fisher with his usual military vim and vigor. Colonel William Lamb commanded the fort. Born September 7, 1835 in Norfolk, Virginia, Colonel Lamb graduated from William and Mary College in Williamsburg, Virginia as a Phi Beta Kappa in 1856. Before the outbreak of the war he edited the *Southern Argus* of Norfolk. At the opening of hostilities, he served on the staff of General Joseph R. Anderson, before being elected colonel of the Thirty-Sixth Regiment of North Carolina troops. The Thirty-Sixth North Carolina eventually became a heavy artillery unit.

During the first year of the war, Major General Samuel French placed Lamb in command of a battery at Fort Anderson, located at Brunswick Point, North Carolina on the Cape Fear River. On July 4, 1862, Lamb took command of Fort Fisher, which guarded Wilmington. The fort was little more than a heap of sand jutting out into the mouth of the Cape Fear River. Colonel Lamb began tearing down the old works and then rebuilding the fort according to his own plans.

As completed by Colonel Lamb, Fort Fisher was almost impregnable. Although not a professionally trained soldier or engineer, Lamb studied many published United States government papers on building forts and their defensive works. Many observers compared Fort Fisher to the Russian fortress of Malakoff at Sebastopol. These types of forts, constructed of earth, could absorb the shock of enemy heavy artillery projectiles, while allowing very little damage to the main structure. Colonel Lamb positioned the gun emplacements on top of thirty-two foot high sand mounds with interior bombproofs. Fort Fisher soon earned the nickname, "The Gibraltar of the South."

Major Reilly spent most of his time readying his regiment and the fort's siege guns. The salt air on the fort's sea face played havoc with the metal guns and their carriages. Reilly's men constantly inspected, cleaned and painted the guns. Reilly also drilled the artillery crews daily and made sure they were prepared, day or night, to man their guns to defend the fort and protect blockade runners from Federal blockading ships.

Strategically located at the mouth of the Cape Fear River, Fort Fisher kept the port city of Wilmington open for much needed supplies, transported from the Bahama Islands, Bermuda and Nova Scotia aboard specially designed block-ade-running ships. During the War Between the States, both the Confederate government and the individual southern states imported necessary supplies and material from Britain. Running these vital supplies through the Yankee blockade was very dangerous, but highly profitable. Many blockade runners came in off the coast of North Carolina, up the Cape Fear River, and onto the Wilmington docks under the protection of Fort Fisher's big guns.

This blockade trade gave Fort Fisher its paramount importance to the Con-federate supply line and the war effort. Major Reilly's responsibilities increased as fear of a Yankee attack by land or by sea mounted. At one point during this time, Major Reilly fell ill with acute bronchitis and was hospitalized in Wilmington. After a week of care in Hospital No. 4, he recovered sufficiently to resume his duties.

The Fort Fisher log book details Major Reilly's struggles with rebellious troops and disease, as well as with maintaining the guns. According to Special Order No. 122, issued July 21, 1864

A garrison court is hereby appointed to meet at Smithville, NC on the twenty-seventh of June 1864 at 11 o'clock a.m. or as soon thereafter as practicable to investigate certain complaints of ill treatment made by Corporal J. Henry Johnson and Private Robert Church of Co. "F" 10th Reg. NCT against Major James Reilly of 10th Reg. NCT and such other cases as may be ordered before it. Detail for the court.

Col. Wm. Lamb, 36th Reg. NCT, Lt. Col. Tail, 40th Reg. NCT, Capt. Wm. Badhaim, Jr., Co. "B" 3rd Batt. Lt. Arty. The court will make and return full and detailed report of this investigation and will declose their opinion on the merits of the cases submitted.

The outcome of this proceeding has remained unknown. The following log book entries detail growing concern for an imminent Federal attack:

Circular
Aug. 22nd, 1864

Indications are that the enemy has made preparations for attacking this point. Commanding officers are called upon to place their works & command in condition at once to resist and repel attacks. They will in person inspect every gun & see that it be in working order. Great watchfulness must be kept up & all unusual movements of the enemy immediately reported.

Circular
Aug. 24th, 1864

The attachments to heavy artillery when manning the guns will have their small arms and ammunition with and near them. Officers are again requested to put the hour as well at which they write their dispatches & communications of importance. When not writing at their respective posts, the locality from which they write will also be stated.

Additional concerns included health issues as stated in the following log entry:

Circular
Oct. 13th, 1864

In consequence of the prevalence of yellow fever at Wilmington, officers & soldiers of this command will not be permitted to visit that place except "on business or under orders."

Several outbreaks of dreaded yellow fever occurred in Wilmington during the war. Few, if any, Wilmington families escaped its grasp. Today, a large section of mass graves at Oakdale Cemetery, used to bury the unfortunate victims, testifies to the severity of yellow fever outbreaks.

By the latter part of October 1864, sixty-four United States Navy warships, commanded by Rear Admiral David Dixon Porter, assembled at Hampton Roads, Virginia in preparation to attack Fort Fisher. The son of Commodore David Porter, a hero of the War of 1812, Admiral Porter was born in Chester, Pennsylvania in 1813. He began his naval career as a cadet in the Mexican navy in 1826 before attending Columbia College in New York. In 1829 he entered the United States Navy as a midshipman on board the *USS Constellation*. In 1835 he passed his midshipman naval examination and in 1841 was commissioned a lieutenant. Porter went on to serve in the Mexican War. By 1864, after participating in several successful naval battles along the Mississippi, he took command of the North Atlantic Blockading Squadron, which patrolled the coasts of Virginia and North Carolina.

The Yankee plan of attack on Fort Fisher was conceived by Major General Benjamin Franklin Butler. Born in Deerfield, New Hampshire in 1818, Butler attended Waterville College in Maine, graduating in 1838. He then made his home in Lowell, Massachusetts and passed the Massachusetts Bar in 1840. Southerners hated General Butler intensely, describing him as a hideous, cross-eyed "beast." Much of this bitterness resulted from his notorious General Order No. 28, issued on May 15, 1862, a few weeks after the Union capture of New Orleans. Order No. 28 stated, "Hereafter when any female shall, by word, gesture or movement, insult or show contempt for any officer or soldier of the United States, she shall be regarded and held liable to be treated as a woman of the town plying her vocation."

General Butler's Order No. 28 drew criticism in the North and in Europe, as well as in the South, earning him the nickname, "Beast" Butler. He was also called "Spoons," for allegedly pilfering silverware from southern homes. By December 1862, public opposition to Butler's harsh methods led to his removal from command of Union forces in New Orleans.

General Butler planned to blow down the earthworks of Fort Fisher and stun the garrison into surrendering by exploding a "powder vessel," a large boat loaded with gunpowder. Under cover of darkness, Union forces would place the powder vessel as close as possible to the walls of the fort and then ignite it. General Grant reluctantly accepted this plan, which was endorsed by Rear Admiral Porter.

Although unaware of these details, the Confederate high command knew that the Yankees were preparing to attack Fort Fisher and reinforced the fort. On December 16, a portion of Company K of the Tenth North Carolina received orders to report to Major Reilly in Wilmington and proceed to Fort Fisher. On December 23, General Whiting ordered Major Reilly to reinforce the fort with two companies of his own regiment, the 40th, containing one hundred and ten men; Company D, 13th North Carolina Battalion with one hundred and fifteen men; and the 7th Battalion Junior Reserves, one hundred and forty in number, placing a grand total of nine hundred men in the fort.

The Junior Reserves were comprised of young men between sixteen and eighteen years old. Portions of these troops had been stationed at Fort Pender, formerly Fort Anderson, and had to cross the Cape Fear River in navy launches and schooners to reach Fort Fisher. Major Reilly assigned the new arrivals quarters, and that night the sounds of fiddles and accordions could be heard throughout the fort. The men sang campfire melodies, such as Dixie, Maryland, My Maryland, Lorena, and a host of other Confederate war songs. However, these men of God also prayed and read their Bibles in preparation for the impending battle.

On Saturday, Christmas Eve 1864, Union Commander A. C. Rhind steered the powder vessel, *USS Louisiana*, loaded with two hundred and fifteen tons of gunpowder, to within fifteen hundred yards of Fort Fisher. After activating an elaborate fuse system, he abandoned the *Louisiana* and returned by launch to the Federal fleet, anchored twelve miles from the fort. At one forty in the morning, the powder vessel exploded without doing any damage to the fort or its garrison. This harmless explosion became known as "Butler's Folly." Only a few officers and men in the fort heard the explosion or felt any impact vibrations. As a result of an unusual atmospheric phenomenon, the explosion was felt and heard in Wilmington, eighteen miles away.

Near dawn, the Union fleet, concealed by a heavy fog, moved into battle formation, positioning its warships in three semi-circles, starting at one half mile to one and one quarter miles from the fort. At twelve forty that afternoon, the Federal fleet opened fire on the fort with over six-hundred heavy guns aboard sixty-four war ships. The *USS Colorado* alone carried fifty-two cannons, outnumbering Fort Fisher's forty-seven guns and mortars. The Yankee fleet pounded Fort Fisher, expending roughly ten thousand projectiles, destroying Colonel Lamb's headquarters and setting several other buildings ablaze.

The Confederate defenders could fire only about one round per gun each half hour, primarily because the heavy smoke from the discharging guns prevented them from seeing their targets. Major Reilly commanded the batteries and troops on the land face of the fort. The batteries on the land face were made up of thirty-two pound seacoast rifled and smoothbore guns, eight and ten-inch Columbiad siege guns and light artillery, including one six-pound Napoleon and two twelve-pound Napoleons.

The land face guns fired primarily at the first circle or line of Federal war ships, located about one half mile offshore and made up of ironclads and wooden warships. Each side inflicted very little damage to the other. The Federal fleet suffered the greatest damage from the accidental bursting of five one hundred pound Parrott rifles aboard their own ships. By late afternoon on the 24th, Major General Whiting entered Fort Fisher to assist Colonel Lamb. Around dusk the Yankee fleet ceased firing and retired to their positions further out to sea.

Early on Sunday, Christmas morning, twenty Union warships shelled the beach area north of Fort Fisher and south of a large sand hill, known as Sugar Loaf, to break open an area for an amphibious landing of Federal infantry. In conjunction with this shelling, the rest of the fleet resumed its bombardment of Fort Fisher. By two in the afternoon, Union infantrymen in john boats hit the beach between Sugar Loaf and Fort Fisher. The first man on the beach, Brigadier General Newton Martin Curtis, was a six foot, seven inch tall native of DePeyster, New York. Curtis graduated from the Gouverneur Wesleyan Seminary and became a postmaster, farmer, lawyer and teacher in DePeyster. In 1861 he volunteered for the Union army and became a captain in the 16th New York Infantry.

Major General Butler commanded the land attack from his headquarters aboard the sidewheel gunboat, *USS Charles Chamberland*. Soon after landing, Curtis' five hundred men from the First Brigade, Second Division, XXIV Army Corps, skirmished with Confederate troops based at Sugar Loaf and commanded by General William Whedbee Kirkland. They quickly overwhelmed Kirkland's troops, capturing several of the Confederates. Kirkland immediately redeployed to the safety of Sugar Loaf to guard the road leading to Wilmington. A native of North Carolina, Kirkland was born at Ayrmont Plantation near Hillsboro in 1833. He attended West Point for three years, but did not graduate. Kirkland accepted a commission as second lieutenant in the United States Marine Corps in 1855.

By three o'clock in the afternoon, with Kirkland's forces out of the way, General Curtis moved south toward Fort Fisher with approximately two hundred and fifty troops from the 142nd New York. He established a reconnaissance post seventy-five yards from the fort's land face. At dusk, Union Lieutenant William Walling climbed a telegraph pole and cut the line running to the north. While atop the pole, Walling confirmed that Fort Fisher was a two-sided fort. He was also able to steal from the outer walls a Confederate garrison flag that had been knocked down during the bombardment. Walling's information convinced General Curtis that the fort could be taken by an infantry assault, but General Butler called a halt to the operation and ordered Curtis to return to the Federal landing zone with his men.

Tempted by the seeming lack of Confederate manpower and with the encouragement of other high ranking officers, Curtis pushed forward to launch a night attack on the northern land face of Fort Fisher. The ever vigilant General Whiting rushed troops from their bombproofs to reinforce Major Reilly at the north land face. Shocked by the sudden heavy blast of Confederate fire power, General Curtis and his troops slowly retreated to the Federal landing zone. Severe weather conditions precluded a safe return by transports to the fleet, stranding General Curtis with six hundred of his men and several hundred Confederate prisoners on the beach for two days. The Confederate prisoners included men from the 17th North Carolina and two hundred and eighteen of General Kirkland's men, captured at Flag Pond.

On December 26, General Butler sailed back to Hampton Roads, leaving Porter's fleet behind. Confederate commanding general, Braxton Bragg, and General Robert F. Hoke arrived at Sugar Loaf late in the afternoon to help reinforce General Kirkland. Instead of attacking and capturing General Curtis' stranded Federal troops on the beach, Bragg allowed the Union fleet to rescue them the following day and sail away. Colonel Lamb ordered his guns to fire a defiant volley at the departing Yankee fleet.

General "Beast" Butler soon learned how the failure of his expedition to capture Fort Fisher infuriated General Grant and Union Secretary of the Navy Gideon Welles. Grant recalled him and within a year Butler resigned in disgrace.

An after-battle report from Major William J. Saunders, Chief of Artillery at Fort Fisher, stated, "If not out of place in this report, I would beg particularly to call attention to the able management of the armament of this fort by the colonel commanding, as also to the skill displayed by that splendid artillerist, Maj. James Reilly, of the Tenth Regiment North Carolina Troops.

The perplexing Braxton Bragg served as commanding officer of the Department of North Carolina in 1864 and 1865. Born in Warrenton, North Carolina in 1817, Bragg was the most controversial of the eight men who reached the rank of full general in the Confederate army. The other seven full generals in service to the Confederate States of America were General Samuel Cooper, General Albert S. Johnston, General Robert E. Lee, General Joseph E. Johnston, General Pierre G. T. Beauregard, General E. Kirby Smith and General John B. Hood.

Bragg graduated from West Point, fifth out of fifty in the Class of 1833. He earned a reputation as a talented organizer, but possessed a quarrelsome personality and was accused by his peers of having caused senseless slaughters, wasted opportunities and a host of disastrous blunders. On several occasions his friendship with President Davis saved him from certain court martial and humiliation.

Bragg's fellow North Carolinian, General Robert Frederick Hoke, was born in

Lincolnton in 1837 and graduated from the Kentucky Military Institute. He died in 1912 in Raleigh and is buried there near the front gate of Oakwood Cemetery.

Immediately following the departure of the Union forces from the vicinity of Fort Fisher in December 1864, General Whiting and Colonel Lamb expressed amazement that the Yankees had given up so easily after such a show of force. They now set about rebuilding and repairing the damage caused by the powerful Union naval bombardment. Gun emplacements, traverses, gun carriages and gun tubes had to be either replaced or repaired. The eight-inch, one hundred and fifty pound Armstrong rifled gun No. 1207, a rare imported British cannon that was mounted at Purdie Battery midway along the sea face, required repair. The center transom was split and the gangway gone, but the carriage was quickly repaired and the gun soon ready for duty. During the attack, the Armstrong gun had fired a one hundred and fifty pound bolt through the boiler of Admiral Porter's flagship, the *USS Malvern*. The Armstrong, a muzzle-loading rifled gun, possessed very high technological advancements and the capability of firing a one hundred and fifty pound specialized steel-studded projectile with great accuracy for up to five miles. The gun tube contained six rifled right hand grooves that could accommodate the steel studs of its projectiles. The gun weighted fifteen thousand seven hundred and thirty-seven pounds and measured one hundred and thirty-one inches, mounted on a mahogany barbette carriage which housed an innovative compressor-braking mechanism to help control the gun's recoil.

Confederate work details cleared hundreds of spent projectiles and shell fragments from inside the fort and along the beach. Unexploded projectiles required special care to prevent them from discharging during the removal process. Confederate crews reconnected the important telegraph line to Sugar Loaf. As they repaired their defenses, the garrison knew it would only be a matter of time before the Yankees would return.

At Hampton Roads, Federal naval forces refitted and reorganized the fleet to make a second attack on Fort Fisher. General Grant assured Admiral Porter that he would send the same troops back to Fort Fisher under a new and more capable commander. His choice for the new commander was Major General Alfred Howe Terry. Born in Hartford, Connecticut in 1827, Terry attended Yale School of Law, but did not graduate, since he had already been admitted to the state bar. A student of the military, Terry eventually made the United States Army his career. He was six feet, two inches tall, described as having a slender build, blue eyes and "bright hair."

Terry's appointment set in motion a campaign that would ultimately decide the fate of the Confederacy. Union transport ships, carrying almost ten thousand Federal soldiers from the Army of the James, left Hampton Roads on the morning of January 6, 1865, bound for Fort Fisher. Admiral Porter, commanding fifty-eight United States warships, left Beaufort, North Carolina on the morning of January 12, to join the Union attacking force. That evening, Colonel Lamb, peering through his telescope from the top of the Fort Fisher ramparts, viewed the lights of the arriving Federal fleet as they appeared one by one on the horizon. General Whiting telegraphed Lamb from Smithville, "The fleet is off Masonborough; be on your guard. I will be with you either inside or out." By seven twenty on the morning of January 13, a division of Yankee gunboats began to shell Federal Point, about four miles north of Fort Fisher, to clear the beach for General Terry's amphibious landing.

General Whiting also telegraphed a special order to Major Reilly at Fort Pender. The order directed Reilly to move his battalion of one hundred and fifty men, consisting of detachments from Company F and Company K of the Tenth North Carolina Artillery, back to Fort Fisher without delay.

The Federal fleet began a powerful, pinpoint artillery bombardment, aiming direct and enfilade fire at Fort Fisher's land face in order to prepare the way for the Union land attack. The Yankees learned from their first attack in December that they had to disable the Confederate guns along the land face for the ground assault to be successful. Because the Union attackers again cut the fort's telegraph lines and because the Confederate siege guns spread large amounts of dense smoke inside the fort, obscuring signal flags, signal corps operators had to move across the Cape Fear River to Smithville in order to keep communications open with Sugar Loaf, from which messages could be relayed to General Bragg in Wilmington.

At eight o'clock on the morning of Friday, January 13, General Terry began his amphibious landing on a narrow sand spit near Myrtle Sound, using hundreds of launches and gigs. Throughout the day, Colonel Lamb received reinforcements made up of artillerymen and Confederate marines, boosting the fort's garrison to fifteen hundred troops. General Whiting and his staff officers arrived by boat at the Battery Buchanan wharf at the south end of Fort Fisher and immediately set out to find Colonel Lamb. When they met, Whiting remarked, "Lamb, my boy, I've come to share your fate. You and your garrison are to be sacrificed." By this time, Whiting had exchanged fruitless telegrams with General Bragg, explaining that Fort Fisher was in great danger and urging him to send more reinforcements.

Bragg, in his typical fashion, did nothing and appeared indifferent to the fort's fate. General Whiting was furious at Bragg's apparent lack of concern for the fort and the lives of its defenders. The only plausible explanation for General Bragg's attitude and inaction is that he might have suffered from an illness, leaving him mentally incapable of making decisions.

Major Reilly and his battalion arrived at Fort Fisher at three o'clock on the morning of Saturday, January 14. Reilly's troops took their positions on the left of the land face, to defend the River Road, Sallyport, and Shepherd's Battery, also called the western salient. By two o'clock that morning, General Terry's troops had already begun digging a line of breastworks to span the width of the peninsula. They built this line to protect themselves from possible attacks by Confederate troops stationed to the north at Sugar Loaf and Wilmington. The Federal line cut Fort Fisher off by land. Confederate troops could now reinforce the fort only by sailing down the Cape Fear River and disembarking at the wharfs at Battery Buchanan.

By late afternoon, Generals Terry and Curtis reconnoitered Fort Fisher's defenses and concluded that the situation was favorable for an all out infantry attack. Admiral Porter agreed with their plan and confirmed that he would put a force of Union sailors and marines ashore to aid in the land attack. As nightfall approached, Porter's fleet began a massive artillery bombardment which lasted throughout the night and disabled almost all of the Confederate guns along Fort Fisher's land face. The Confederates tried in vain to remount their guns and repair their works, but the constant heavy artillery fire forced them undercover. Major Reilly estimated that the Union fleet fired one hundred or more shells per minute into Fort Fisher.

Sunday, January 15, 1865 was a clear, cold morning with calm seas. The Union fleet began another punishing bombardment of the land face in preparation for General Terry's attack. By this time only two eight-inch Confederate Columbiad guns, located on each flank of the land face, remained operational. At the apex of the Union bombardment, General Johnson Hagood's reinforcements, men from the Eleventh and Twenty-Fifth South Carolina Regiments in General Hoke's Division, arrived at the wharfs of Battery Buchanan. Under murderous fire from the Union fleet, these troops made their way through the mile and three quarter gauntlet to the Confederate fort land face.

Brigadier General Adelbert Ames's division of Union infantry made their final preparations for the assault while Colonel Galusha Pennypacker and Colonel Louis Bell landed their brigades near the vicinity of Craig's Landing to join

General Curtis's brigade. General Terry had established his command post five hundred yards north of Fort Fisher's land face at Battery Holland. The attack began as Union skirmishers moved forward and Admiral Porter's two thousand two hundred and sixty-one man contingent of marines and sailors landed on the beach roughly one and one half mile north of the land face. This force, commanded by Captain K. R. Breese, was made up of men from thirty-five different Union warships, who had never before operated as a combat unit, but were delighted to be off their ships and free from the rigors of sea life.

General Terry dispatched a detachment of the Thirteenth Indiana sharp-shooters, armed with new breechloading lever-action Spencer repeating rifles to join the attack. The Spencers held seven rounds, allowing them to outfire the Confederate muzzle loading muskets by a ratio of seven to one. About three hundred yards north of the land face, General Curtis ordered his brigade forward with Pennypacker and Bell forming on his rear.

By this time only three hundred and fifty of General Hagood's South Caro-linians had made their way to the land face. Colonel Lamb commanded a total force of only nineteen hundred Confederates, defending Fort Fisher against overwhelming odds and massive naval artillery fire. Before arriving at the fort, General Whiting had repeatedly telegraphed General Bragg, literally begging the delusional commander to come to their aid, but his efforts fell on deaf ears. General Bragg apparently never grasped the seriousness of the situation at Fort Fisher.

At three twenty-five in the afternoon, the Yankee warship *USS Malvern* sounded an ear-splitting blast from its steam whistle, followed by whistles from the entire Union fleet, given as a signal to commence the land attack. When the Federal naval bombardment abruptly stopped, Colonel Lamb sensed the imminent Union attack along the land face and rushed his troops into position to repel the advancing Yankees. The troops emerged from their bombproofs, which were dug into the sand bastions and mounds. Major Reilly, with two hundred and fifty of his North Carolinians, defended the left flank, or western salient, consisting of the River Road sallyport and Slough Bridge, which were considered the weakest points in the fort's defenses. Colonel Lamb, with five hundred troops, commanded the northeast bastion and the main sallyport. General Whiting positioned the remaining force along the ramparts and traverses nearer to the sea face and adjacent to the northeast bastion.

Without waiting for orders, Union Captain Breese launched a wild headlong charge along the beachfront at Fort Fisher's northeast bastion. The Union sailors and leathernecks rushed forward armed only with cutlasses and revolvers. Colonel Lamb unleashed devastating artillery fire into their ranks. General Whiting, in his usual defiant style, stood on top of the ramparts, cursing the enemy and urging his men to, "kill those damn Yankees!" The Union attackers suffered severe losses, and their retreat disintegrated into a rout. Colonel Lamb noticed a particularly reckless and brave Union naval officer in the assaulting column, who seemed to lead the charge. Lamb ordered his troops to pick off this officer to discourage and disorganize the assailants. This officer would later be identified to Lamb as Captain James Parker of the United States Navy. As Breese's attack melted in confusion, the Confederate defenders along the northeast bastion gave a wild cheer. In the midst of this celebration, General Whiting and Colonel Lamb were shocked to see Union flags waving over the fort's western salient.

In conjunction with the assault on the northeast bastion, General Adelbert Ames ordered one of his brigades, commanded by General Curtis, to begin the attack on the western salient. Curtis's troops moved at the run and charged headlong at the salient, where Major Reilly waited for them. Reilly's troops opened fire with small arms and poured devastating canister fire into the Union flanks with a twelve-pound Napoleon smoothbore gun from the sallyport gate and a Parrott rifle near the river marsh. Under this heavy fire about one hundred of Curtis's men reached the fort's palisades. Armed with heavy axes, they began to chop holes in the palisades' wooden walls. Unfortunately, Major Reilly had posted his men on the floor of the gun emplacements, thus limiting their field of vision and giving the Yankees an area safe from Confederate fire. Because of the height and width of the fort's works, the Confederates could not see the Federals until they moved out of the safe zone and began to climb the parapets. Once the breech was made, Curtis ordered his men forward and Yankees began pouring through the holes chopped in the palisades. Fierce and desperate hand-to-hand fighting erupted as the Union troops moved through the walls of the western salient. Major Reilly's Confederates and Major Curtis's bluebellies cursed and shouted as they clubbed each other with pistols and musket butts, and slashed and stabbed with their bayonets. Meanwhile, the Federal naval guns resumed firing, engaging the fort's sea face guns in a fierce artillery duel. The horrendous noise and confusion prevented men and officers on both sides from coordinating, communicating or maintaining any semblance of order. Fighting desperately, the Confederates failed to hold back the Union assault at the fort's weakest points, the sallyport and the riverside gate. The guns at Battery Buchanan on the far southern end of the Fort Fisher peninsula then unleashed long range artillery fire into the rear of the western salient, killing and wounding friend and foe alike.

Colonel Galusha Pennypacker planted the Union colors of the Ninety-Seventh Pennsylvania on the third traverse of the land face, but immediately received a severe wound, as all eight of his officers were cut down. Major Reilly and his Confederates slowly retreated along the traverse and onto the fort's parade ground below the battlements. Colonel Louis Bell's Union brigade crossed the Wilmington Road Causeway, rushing into the battlements to support their comrades. Over four thousand Yankee troops now gathered on the slopes, base and walls of the western salient and surged onto the parade ground. The Union standard bearers hurried to plant their flags along the ramparts, and soon the colors of the Fourth New Hampshire, Thirteenth Indiana, One Hundred and Sixty-Ninth New York and One Hundred and Fifteenth New York floated prominently over the land face near the third traverse.

General Whiting indignantly pushed up the third traverse to snatch down one of the hated Yankee flags. As he grappled with the Federal color bearer, the Yankee troops noticed his insignia and demanded his surrender. Whiting screamed defiantly, "Go to hell, you Yankee bastards!" Just at that moment, two bullets hit his right thigh. Several of Whiting's men pulled him to safety and rushed him to the fort's bombproof hospital below the "pulpit," located near the sea face. Chaos continued with the hottest and most prolonged fighting of the day, as men fought like demons, kicking, gouging, stabbing, and stepping on the dead, the wounded, and the blood soaked ground to get at each other.

Colonel Lamb stood on the open plane of the fort's parade ground, approximately one hundred and fifty feet from the enemy. He knew that he and his men had very few options remaining. The tide of battle had turned and the Federals were already starting to entrench their positions as night approached. Lamb realized the need for a powerful counterattack to prevent the enemy from erecting strong defensive breastworks. He passed the word down the line to all his officers and men, and all agreed to follow him.

Lamb sprang to his feet and ordered, "Charge bayonets." Waving his sword, he shouted above the din of battle, "Forward, double quick, march." Just as the men rose up, Colonel Lamb was sent to his knees by a bullet in his left hip and the charge immediately fell apart. His men carried Lamb to the hospital at the "pulpit," where surgeons determined that blood loss left him unable to resume command.

About four thirty that afternoon Colonel Lamb sent his adjutant, Lieutenant John M. Kelly, to find Major Reilly. When Reilly arrived at the hospital, Lamb informed him that, as the only senior officer fit for duty, he would take command of Fort Fisher. Major Reilly assumed command and promised Colonel Lamb

157

that he would continue to fight as long as humanly possible.

Major Reilly led his men in a gallant, but hopeless, fight for the rest of the day. Unfortunately, despite their most heroic efforts, the overwhelming number of Union troops pushed Reilly and his men southward, down the peninsula. Reilly later recalled, "I saw there was not a possible chance of defending ourselves." Out of options, he sent Captain Alfred Crippen Van Benthuysen to the "pulpit" hospital. The brave captain barely had enough time to evacuate General Whiting and Colonel Lamb by stretcher. Major Reilly and his dwindling band of men retreated to Battery Buchanan at the far southern end of Fort Fisher with Whiting and Lamb in tow. Earlier that afternoon, Reilly had taken the precaution of dispatching Captain Zachariah Adams with orders to Captain Robert T. Chapman and his naval force to hold their position at Battery Buchanan. Chapman's force provided Reilly's last ray of hope to escape Fort Fisher, using the boats docked at the battery's wharves. That evening, Captain Chapman, hearing rumors that the fort had fallen, decided to disobey Reilly's orders and save himself and his men. Chapman's boats pulled away just as the first of Reilly's men appeared on the wharf. "Old Tarantula" was furious that he, Colonel Lamb, General Whiting and their men had been abandoned by Captain Chapman. The departing Confederate sailors and marines had also spiked the battery's large seacoast guns, rendering them useless. Major Reilly now had no choice but to surrender. One can only imagine the Irish cursing he expounded on Captain Chapman for leaving the fort's defenders to the mercy of the rapidly advancing Yankee columns.

CHAPTER IX

THE FALL OF FORT FISHER

Two post-war personal accounts of Major Reilly's actions and the surrender of Fort Fisher give different perspectives on the events of Sunday, January 15, 1865. On October 27, 1893, Captain E. Lewis Moore of Framingham, Massachusetts, addressed a letter to Mayor S. H. Fishblate of Wilmington, North Carolina, which was published in the November 3 edition of the *Wilmington Weekly Star*. It read:

> *Sir — I shall be glad to know whether Major James Reilly who commanded a battalion of North Carolina artillery during two attacks on Fort Fisher is still living and where I shall address him or if any of his living representatives can be communicated with by me.*
>
> *I am in possession of the sword (saber) that he wore so honorably in both those engagements and which I received from his own hand on the surrender of the fort. I shall be most happy to send it to him by express if he wishes to reclaim it.*
>
> *I shall be pleased to have his recollections of our brief meeting on that memorable evening.*

> *E. Lewis Moore,*
> *Late Captain and*
> *Assistant Adjutant General*
> *Volunteers,*
> *Abbott's Brigade*
> *7th Connecticut*

Major Reilly replied, requesting that the sword be sent "collect," writing:

> *You, my brave and gallant opponent in war, fully illustrate the magnanimous character of a good soldier and gentleman. I fought you with a determination that afternoon*

(from the time Gen. Whiting and Col. Lamb were wounded, about 3 o'clock pm., command devolved on me) that would be hard to excel, but it was like unto a mole and a mountain — uphill work. Your troops were all around my gallant little band of Tarheels, fighting from traverse to traverse, with no hope but fighting to the last ditch. At dark, when I fell back from Fisher, I had only forty-four men and two officers with me. I formed my little command and moved to Battery Buchanan. When I saw the condition of affairs I called Maj. Hill and Capt. Van Benthuysen, and held a consultation and came to a conclusion to surrender. After waiting some time I observed the skirmish line of your troops advancing toward the point. We went forward about three hundred yards and stopped. I took my handkerchief and placed it upon the point of my saber and awaited your coming, when the surrender was made about 8 o'clock p.m. It was a distressing time to us. When I surrendered my saber to you it was with a heart of the deepest depression. As a brave soldier you treated us courteously, and showed no bravado over our defeat for which accept my sincere thanks. Of the other officers that were with me on that memorable occasion Major Hill is dead and I have not heard from Capt. Van Benthuysen since the surrender. Captain, if you have time come to see me, and we will visit the fort and see its ruins.

Ezra Lewis Moore was born in Lyme, London County, Connecticut in 1834. He graduated from the State Normal School of Connecticut in New Britain in 1856. Following the outbreak of the War Between the States, Moore enlisted as a private in Company G, Seventh Connecticut Infantry. The company descriptive book lists him as twenty-seven years old, five feet eight inches in height, with blue eyes and light hair and complexion. He was promoted to adjutant of the regiment with the rank of first lieutenant in 1863 and participated in the second Battle of Fort Fisher in January 1865.

It is odd that Captain Moore never spoke of his role in the initial surrender of Fort Fisher in letters that he sent home immediately after the battle, nor did he mention it in explanatory notes which he prepared after the war, using his letters and other sources. The published history of the Seventh Connecticut, which drew heavily on Moore's writings, made no mention of the incident.

Captain Moore, a loyal officer, dutifully supported his commander, General Ames, who earned two stars and a commendation from Congress for "his" victory. This action may have cost Moore recognition for his role in the surrender. Perhaps Captain Moore's awareness of the negative impact of excessive braggadocio compelled him to keep his notoriety to himself and avoid public ridicule and criticism during the post-war years when no fewer than six Federal officers claimed to have received Fort Fisher's surrender. A farmer, teacher, state legislator and businessman after the war, Captain Moore passed away in 1911 at his home in Framingham, Massachusetts from heart disease.

Adding to the confusion surrounding Major Reilly's surrender of Fort Fisher, Reilly himself wrote a detailed second version for publication in a local newspaper. The following version, reprinted in its entirety and with annotations, is from an original handwritten manuscript in the William L. DeRosset Papers, 1862-1904, North Carolina State Archives:

ACCOUNT OF FALL OF FORT FISHER

James Reilly
Late Maj. Regt. Arty. N.C. S. T.

I saw it stated that Col. Lamb was in command of Fort Fisher when it was captured. Such is not the case. Please make this correction. I was in command of the Fort after the chivalrous Whiting, and the brave Lamb were wounded- Both of those officers were wounded about the same time, Whiting first and Lamb shortly after. This sad occurrence happened about 3:00 in the afternoon. I being the Senior Officer then for duty - the command devolved on me, and under the circumstances I was placed in a very disagreeable situation, But I assumed it with all its responsibility and with a small number of brave men. (I never had over one hundred men fighting after the first assault, and that number dwindled down to about thirty two (32) before 8:00 P.M.) kept the heavy assaulting column of the enemy in check all that memorable afternoon. The men that did fight, fought as well as any men ever fought. Shortly after the enemy got possession of the western angle of the work the fleet slackened its fire to a very great extent. This encouraged our men and I revived considerable enthusiasm and determination amongst them and it showed plainly that they meant business and the few that did come out of the chambers where they were seeking protection from the destructive and murderous fire of the enemy fleet all day fought as men ought to fight for the protection of Hearths and Homes. I availed myself of this cessation of shot and formed about one hundred and fifty men in the open space near the sally port. As soon as the formation was complete I advanced on a body of the enemy that established themselves in the open space between the western angle of the Fort and the river. This body annoyed us very much all the after-noon. I put one of the S.Ca. Regt. Colours by my side and in front of the column. As soon as the enemy observed our object they opened a very destructive fire on our advance Column. Under such a fire our men began to waver and fall back, and by the time I reached near the angle of the work I had not sixty men with me, the balance who was not killed or wounded took shelter behind the Traverses and in the Sally Port. In this last effort to expel the enemy I lost heavily and that brave and gallant soldier who carried the colours was killed by my side. His loss created some confusion in the attack and I was compelled to fall back but without apparent confusion, to the sand bank in front of the main magazine. When I reformed and kept up as Heavy and as Destructive a fire on the enemy as my small command would admit throughout the whole fight. In this effort I was ably assisted by Capts. Baker & Brady, (the former belonged to a S.C. Regt. My orderly) [Captain W. B. Baker, Co. L, Twenty-first South Carolina; Captain Kinchen J. Braddy, Second Co. C Thirty-sixth NC (Braddy's Battery), imprisoned at Fort Columbus, New York] *– acted as brave soldiers and some other officers who I regret I do not know. Lieut. Arendell,* [First Lieutenant Thomas Arendell, Co. F, Tenth North Carolina, imprisoned at Fort Columbus, New York] *and my adjt. Lt. Fuller* [probably Second Lieutenant Irvin Fulford, Co. K, Tenth North Carolina, imprisoned at Fort Columbus, New York] *of the Tenth N.C.S.T. Act. Segt Madell.* [Pvt. Samuel L] *Dill* [Co.K, Tenth NC] *& Pvt. C. Will* [Private Charles T. Willis, Co. K, Tenth North Carolina] *is done good service during the whole after noon. The former took his musket and used it very effectively, besides encouraging several of his own Company Pvts. Pate* [four Pate brothers in Co. F, Tenth North Carolina, imprisoned at Elmira, New York], *Hobbs* [Corporal George A. Hobbs, Co. K, Tenth North Carolina] *& others who rallied about him. His conduct has good effect on the* [illegible] *Troop and kept them to their work pretty well- The fighting was very close and severe with shot and shell, and had a very demoralizing effect on the men that was fighting in the open space behind the sand bank and exposed to quite a terrible fire, not with standing the great effort on the part of the enemy they were not able to dislodge us, until after dark and the moon raised when I found myself nearly surrounded, this little band was completely broke down after fighting nearly all day but there was no surrender written on their face. After I reform my line with my left well up the old* [illegible] *breast work so as to enable me to give a direct fire on the works and in command of Capt.(James L. McCormic) McCormick*[sic] [Captain James L. McCormick, Co. D, First Battalion, North Carolina Heavy Artillery], *that gallant officer was killed at his post. Peace to his ashes. He displayed courage and ability and kept his men well in hand up to the time of his death, about this time a white flag was displayed from the sally-port. I could not understand what it meant, as I knew the enemy did not get that far down the work, at the solicitation of some of the officers I ceased firing and took my handkerchief and gave it to Capt. Brady, who put* [it] *on the point of his sword. I ordered him to advance towards the sally-port (& see what was wanted) as soon as the firing ceased, and everything quiet. To my surprise our men came out and instead of coming toward us they ran towards the enemy. As soon as I observed there object I recalled*

Capt. Brady and commenced firing (I know I gained considerable advantage by keeping up a constant and as steady a fire on the enemy as I could. It kept them from making any formation whatever for the continuation of the assault, and they were content to keep behind the captured works and would not make any demonstration until after dark). And the men fought with more determination than ever, and my gallant troops was greatly incensed at the dastardly conduct of there comrades. I maintained my position until about seven P.M. under cover of darkness the enemy made their formation and made the attack simultaneously at several points. This concentrated attack compelled me to fall back from one position to another until we were driven from the fort, not However until sometime after I sent Genl. Whiting & Col. Lamb to Battery Buchanon with the expectation that they would be able to get over the River, as I was under the impression that Capt. Chapman [Captain Robert T. Chapman, CS Navy] had everything in readiness to render what assistance he could (for He & portion of his command was not employed during the day that I am aware of) in getting our wounded officers & men away from the Battery. After allowing sufficient time to elapse for the officers before mentioned to get away I formed my brave little command of thirty two into a column of fours, and the brave men who did the last fighting near (?) Head Quarters at Fort Fisher with the Cool & Brave Capt. Powell [Captain John R. Powell, Co. C, 3rd Battery North Carolina Light Artillery, imprisoned at Fort Columbus, New York], the gallant Arendell & Lieut. M (?) [Lieutenant J. Campbell Murdoch, Co. C, CS Marines, imprisoned at Fort Columbus, New York] of the Marine Corps with saddened Hearts marched away from the fort we defended with all our might. In fact from the superior force & fire we had to contend against that whole afternoon I consider the defense one of the most determined of the war. It was from Traverse to Traverse, from Traverse to main magazine, from there to the Brest [sic] work where the last and most determined stand was made, and did not leave until we were attacked on both flank & front. I wish I could know the names of the Thirty two men who stood by me that evening. Well might their names be put on the Roll of Honor of the N. C. Troops, for none fought more gallantly or with more determination or valour. Our march was directed to Battery Buchanon, where I expected to reform our shattered [?] ranks, and to be in a position to engage the enemy under more favorable circumstance. The command was badly disorganized from the position they were placed in and the mode of fighting we had to resort to, then were subject to the demoralizing effect of the destructive fire of the enemies fleet (which a portion of the time fired over one hundred shots per minute into the fort. I was ordered by Genl. Whiting to count the number on several occasions myself) and the land forces I was fully confident I would be able to reorganize for when I came within sight of the Battery. I halted my little column, for two objectives, First to see if we were pursued, second to inform Capt. Chapman as I presumed he was in a

163

position to render me what assistance I needed by having his men and armament ready for action, and on my approach to the Battery not to fire on us. For this reason when I halted I sent Capt. Powell to the Battery with a verbal message to Capt. Chapman not to fire on any organized body approaching the work. I was confident Chapman was still in the Battery for I thought him too good a soldier to abandon us, for we were sailing in the same ship and let us all go down together. What still gave me more confidence was that [end of page 3 of manuscript].

I sent Capt. Adams [Captain Zachariah T. Adams, Co. D, 13th Battery, North Carolina Light Artillery, imprisoned at Fort Columbus, New York] a gallant officer to him about 4 P.M. with a verbal message to this effect not to abandon the Battery for when I was forced out of Fort Fisher I would fall back on Buchanon and fight the enemy there. Capt. Adams returned to me and said he saw Capt. Chapman and gave me as a reply 'very well.' But what surprise and mortification came upon me when Capt. Powell returned and informed me that Capt. Chapman & command was gone with few exception the Battery was abandoned and the guns spiked, and on my advance I found about six hundred officer & men perfectly [?] disorganized. With considerable effort of myself and several officers we succeeded in getting their Battery [?] re-organized but three fourths of them had no arms, & we had no means at that hour of the night of procuring any or of defending our position against an organized and victorious enemy. We had a splendid opportunity to retrieve [?], our defeat [?] and get away. If the armament of the Battery had been service-able. It was as bright as day the enemy advancing on the two fronts of the Battery, with our guns pouring shell and canister on them as they advanced down the sandy plain. Our men free from the destructive and demoralizing effect of the fire from the fleet, with the officers in charge of their respective commands and that their men kept a well directed fire of musketry on the lines as they came within range and advanced. The whole mode of fighting was changed. We would have regained courage and the enemy would not have captured us, not that night at all events for the position was very strong. And I always have been confident we were able to hold it I could have communicated with Genl. Hebert [General Louis Hebert] and get [illegible] for there was plenty at his disposal at Fort Pender, for to get all the troops across the river. I knew from the activity the enemy displayed in the latter part of the attack on the fort that they would soon advance upon and attack Buchanon and as soon as they would come within range they would open fire on a defenseless mass. When I saw there was not a possible chance of defending ourselves, I took Maj. Hill [Major James H. Hill, Whiting's Adjutant] and Capt. Van Benthusen [sic] [Captain Alfred C. Van Benthuysen, CS Marines, severely wounded] of the Marine Corps, and went some distance in advance of the Battery and awaited their coming. We had a white flag with us and met the enemies skirmish line under the command of *Capt. Eldridge* [Reilly appears to refer to Captain Daniel Eldredge, Third N.H., who later wrote the history of that regiment. Eldredge actually had been wounded and returned north and was not present at the second Battle of Fort Fisher. Reilly probably meant Capt. J. Homer Edgerly of the Third N.H.] *and I told that officer we surrendered and requested him to halt and retire his line and not to let them fire on our defenseless troops. Capt. Eldridge with the instinct of a true soldier he complied with my request and reported I think to Genl. Abbott who came up and was conducted by Maj. Hill to Genl. Whiting. This is a mere detail account for the time I was in command of the fort during the assault of the enemy, the operations and surrender of Fort Fisher It was immaterial to me who commanded. I went there with my Battalion to fight knowing there was a trusted leader, the gallant Whiting, in command. I saw him tried on a hard fought field, and history wants a true record of this event of our late struggle, and I give it impartial so that hereafter it may be correctly known who was in command on that memorable afternoon and who surrendered Fort Fisher. I did it not from any cause or act, of my own, but for the want of fighting material to defend the most important of our sea coast defenses — It is not my desire to detract one Iota from the reputation Col Lamb made for himself whilst in command of Fort Fisher for so far as I know he was a good officer. But it has been so often repeated by the press that he was in command at the time, I think it proper to give a correct statement of the fact from the time Col. Lamb was wounded, and I officially notified of the fact by Maj. Hill and directed as Senior Officer for duty to assume command of the Fort.*

There were several acts of bravery performed by both officers and men during the day. For instance, Lt. Hazell [Lieutenant William Hassell, Third Co. G, 40th NC, imprisoned at Fort Columbus, New York] *in command of a detachment of men in one* [of] *the gun platforms, took his musket during the assault and by his conduct and behavior encouraged his men & they fought during the time very well as he inspired confidence in them by his gallantry. Another instance came to my knowledge of a marine, an Irishman by the name of Fitz — Patrick observed a crowd of the enemy collecting in the open plateau between the redoubt and the Fort. He came to me several times about the matter. He was so persistent that I went with him. I saw a crowd of about fifteen (Then afterwards they were in the act of removing Genl. Galusha Pennypacker who was wounded during the assault I called the Ord. Segt. And got a lanyard & some free men for him and told him to go and select one of the guns between where we were standing & the salient angle of the works. That was not badly disabled double shot it with canister and report to me and we would fire at the crowd. He quickly…as ordered He worked the gun and I pointed it. As soon as it was ready he discharged it I going to the windward side to observe the effect of the fire. It was very good and it done him so much good to see the crowd scatter and some of them left wounded. He forgot everything else and the risk he was running for both transom of the carriage was shattered by an envalade* [sic] *shot. The right transom ben* [being?] *. the shortest and from the recoil of the gun, carriage and gun went over the platform. Ah may if it was not for the gun going over we would have got some of them, as it was we got a few. They left their genl there. They were very careful how they crossed the plateau the whole evening afterwards. It was the last heavy gun fired from the Fort. There was several more acts of bravery the names of the gallant officers and men who performed them I do not know. At the last traverse we fought at the enemy was one side and we the other — I directed my men to stand firm. I was on the ground between two traverses pistol in hand. I heard the officer in command on the other side encourage his men by directing them to move forward - As soon as they appeared above the top of the traverse I discharged my six shots at them (& from what I could learn wounded the officer),* [This was Edgerly. Reilly actually did not wound him] *drove them back then I formed my little column and doubled quick very regularly to the main magazine where I took a position and opened a well directed fire on the assaulting column that was approaching me from the sally port and made them take shelter behind the traverses — By giving this statement publication in the columns of your valuable paper you will oblige, yours respectfully.*

Jas. Reilly
Late Maj. 10th Regt. Arty, N.C.S.T.

Major James H. Hill reported to General Whiting as his adjutant on October 2, 1861. He served with Whiting from the Peninsula Campaign of 1862 until the fall of Fort Fisher.

James Hoffman Hill was born at Hancock's Barracks, Maine in 1834, where his father, Colonel Joseph Hill, was stationed. James's mother was a Hoffman, a descendant of a Revolutionary War general. James Hill graduated from West Point in 1855 and served with Captain Barnard Bee on the Utah Expedition.

When the southern states declared their independence, Lieutenant Hill and Captain Bee resigned their United States Army positions. Hill was appointed first lieutenant of artillery by South Carolina and reported for duty in Virginia under General Joseph E. Johnston. He rejoined his friend Bee, who was now a general, as assistant adjutant general and took part in the Battle of First Manassas, where he was wounded and Bee was killed. In October 1861 Hill received the rank of major and became adjutant general to General William H. C. Whiting, with whom he served from the Peninsula Campaign until the fall of Fort Fisher.

Major Hill's wife, Mary McRee Walker, and General Whiting's wife, Katherine Davis Walker, were sisters. After Fort Fisher's surrender, Hill was imprisoned at Fort Columbus, New York and exchanged on February 25, 1865 at City Point, Virginia. After the end of the war, he returned to Wilmington, where he engaged in the mercantile business. In 1870 he was employed as freight agent for the W. C. & A. Railroad. He moved to Richmond to take a position as chief of the baggage department of the Associated Railways of the Carolinas. In December 1889 he became ill with typhoid fever and pneumonia and returned to Wilmington under the care of his nephew, J. Bolles. He died there the following year at age fifty-seven. He and his wife are buried at Oakdale Cemetery in Wilmington, North Carolina.

Captain Alfred Crippen Van Benthuysen had an extremely interesting and colorful military career. Born in Bedford, Long Island, now part of Brooklyn, New York, about 1837, but raised in New Orleans, Van Benthuysen reportedly fought in the Tai-Ping Rebellion in China in the late 1850s and served with Guiseppe Garibaldi and General Avezzana in the movement to unite Italy in 1860. He accompanied Garibaldi on his triumphant entry into Rome.

By May 1861 he had returned to Louisiana and was appointed captain in the Confederate Marine Corps. Van Benthuysen enjoyed high placed connections in the Confederate government. His aunt, Eliza, married Joseph Davis, a brother of President Jefferson Davis. Despite these connections and his credible performance under fire, Van Benthuysen repeatedly had difficulties with fellow officers. He faced court martial twice in 1862, while serving in Virginia; both times President Davis suspended his sentence.

By June 1863 he transferred to Mobile, Alabama, where he received a telegram, offering him the choice of returning to Virginia or taking a command at Wilmington. He chose Wilmington and reported to General Whiting.

He took part in both battles of Fort Fisher and was wounded in the head during the second Union assault. He received a special commendation for transporting the wounded General Whiting and Colonel Lamb to Battery Buchanan. Shipped North as a wounded prisoner of war, Van Benthuysen was hospitalized at Fort Columbus, New York and exchanged in February 1865 at City Point, Virginia. March 7 found him on duty at the Richmond-Drewry's Bluff area as part of the defense of the Petersburg line. Van Benthuysen accompanied President Davis on his flight south after the evacuation of Richmond. He joined the president's baggage wagons as they left Charlotte, North Carolina on April 26, 1865. When the wagon train split into two groups near Sandersonville, Georgia, Van Benthuyesen stayed with the group that headed to Florida. Unable to continue as a military unit due to the Federal pursuit, the group decided to divide the gold from the Confederate treasury. Van Benthuysen reportedly received four hundred gold sovereigns worth one thousand nine hundred and forty dollars and an additional fifty-five dollars for travel expenses. He was paroled at Baldwin, Florida near the end of May 1865. Returning to New Orleans, he married Rosario (Rose) Trezevant. He died on November 15, 1871 in New Orleans, and is buried in Lafayette Cemetery Number One in the Garden District of New Orleans, Louisiana.

Capt. Edgerly recalled that during the attack at the mound battery, "I was on the run for the flag with a dozen or more men at my heels. Arriving at the flag-staff, and meeting with no serious resistance, I hastily cut the halliards; and in a twinkling the flag was in my possession, and I and my men on the way back to rejoin the main body." Edgerly stated that one of the captured rebel officers, probably Major Reilly, told him that he had snapped his revolver three times at him during the engagement.

Lieutenant Robert T. Chapman of Alabama attended the United States Naval Academy from 1853 to 1857. Commissioned lieutenant in 1855, Chapman resigned from the United States Navy in January 1861 to join the Confederate Navy. He served aboard the CSS Sumter under the command of the famous naval officer Raphael Semmes and then served aboard the CSS Georgia. During the summer of 1864, at great personal risk, he took direct orders from Confederate Secretary of State Judah P. Benjamin to smuggle the great seal of the Confederacy from England, through the Yankee blockade and deliver it to the Confederate capital. Arriving in London, he reported to James M. Mason, the Confederate commissioner in England. The great seal was produced by the Wyon firm, chief engravers for Queen Victoria, at a cost of six hundred dollars. Lieutenant Chapman had a special valise made to carry the seal through the blockade. He placed several pounds of lead in the valise so that it would sink to the ocean floor if he was ever in danger of being captured.

Lieutenant Chapman returned to America on the Cunard Liner Africa from Liverpool to Halifax. He then sailed to Bermuda on board the Alpha and ran the blockade into Wilmington. Becoming seriously ill, he entrusted the seal to his good friend, Lieutenant Campbell, who delivered it to Secretary Benjamin in Richmond.

On duty at Fort Fisher by November 1864, Lieutenant Chapman received a promotion to the rank of captain. Colonel Lamb's diary recounts that on December 3, 1864, "Capt. Chapman, of Battery Buchanan played a joke on Major Venable and Mr. Bowers which might have been serious. He had them waylaid on their way to his battery by a party who pretended they were a yankee raiding party. An alarm was made, long roll of the drums was beat, etc."

Captain Chapman performed bravely during the first Union attack on December 24 and 25, 1864. Although his retreat from Battery Buchanan up the Cape Fear River during the second attack on January 15, 1865 remains controversial, there are no records to indicate that he was ever brought up on any charges. After the fall of the Confederacy, he was paroled at Gainesville, Alabama on June 19, 1865. He moved to Wharton County, Texas, where he joined the Buchel Camp of the United Confederate Veterans and was honored for his service to the Confederacy. Captain Chapman practiced law in Texas until his death in 1905 and is buried in the Old City Cemetery in Galveston, Texas.

Major Reilly has left historians quite a dilemma as to the events surrounding the surrender of Fort Fisher. This author believes that it is possible that Reilly surrendered to both Captain Moore and Captain Edgerly. Reilly states that two Union columns approached Battery Buchanan, spread out and separated by some distance. He may have surrendered to the closest approaching column in order to protect his men, then seeing through the darkness and confusion a second column drawing near, decided to avoid further casualties by surrendering to the second column. These events will remain a historical mystery unless more facts surface. Regardless, according to military protocol, the highest ranking officer had to officially surrender the fort, so the official surrender took place when the wounded General Whiting gave the fort over to Union generals Terry and Ames. The January 1865 Battle of Fort Fisher remained the largest joint amphibious assault in American military history until the Allied invasion of Normandy on June 6, 1944. Union forces fired an estimated 40,000 projectiles at the Confederate fort during the battles of December 1864 and January 1865.

After the surrender of Fort Fisher, Union steamships transported the captured Confederate officers to northern prisons. The Union transports, *USS Governor Chase* and *USS California*, took General Whiting and Colonel Lamb, both wounded, to separate locations. Lamb sailed aboard the *California* en route to Fort Delaware, but a severe winter storm had frozen the river approach to the fort. The *California* was then rerouted to Fort Columbus, New York. After being placed on board the *California*, Lamb was surprised by a visit from Captain James Parker, the reckless and brave officer who had led the Union naval attack on the northeast bastion, and who Lamb had ordered his men to pick off. Now Colonel Lamb expressed gratitude that such a courageous foe had escaped unarmed. When Parker found out that Lamb was a resident of Norfolk, Virginia, he arranged to have him put ashore at nearby Fort Monroe. There, Lamb entered the Chesapeake Federal Hospital.

General Whiting boarded the *Governor Chase* at Fort Fisher en route to Fort Monroe, but was transferred to the *USS DeMolay* and taken to Fort Columbus. Confederate surgeon Spiers Singleton tended to General Whiting's wounds during the seven-day voyage north, but in spite of this care, Whiting's health worsened during the trip. Whiting was imprisoned along with a number of other Confederate officers from Fort Fisher at Fort Columbus on Governor's Island in New York harbor.

Major Reilly arrived at Fort Delaware before the winter storm had closed the area to shipping. This fort was located on tiny Pea Patch Island, in the Delaware River at the mouth of Delaware Bay. Reilly was held in Division #27, while a prisoner at Fort Delaware. During his imprisonment, he received a surprise visit from his old artillery commander and friend from United States Army days, Union General Henry J. Hunt. We can only imagine the conversations and stories that must have passed between these two men who had not met in person since before the war, but had faced each other across many battlefields. General Hunt completely surprised Reilly when he offered him an opportunity to rejoin the United States Army as a commissioned officer. Major Reilly never accepted this kind offer. Hunt arranged for Reilly to receive special treatment and privileges not usually given to prisoners of war.

General Hunt often commented that most gentlemen of the old United States Army held concepts of honor, charity and tolerance. Men like General McClellan, whom Hunt viewed as the epitome of these gentlemanly concepts, hoped to bring the Confederacy to the peace table and work out honorable terms to end the war. As the war progressed, a rising group of "Lincoln Men," including Generals Sherman and Sheridan, embraced total warfare, not only to preserve the Union but to destroy the Confederacy and its army and to wipe out and uproot all vestiges of southern culture and society. By vanquishing and annihilating the entire southern civilization, these leaders advocated destroying the very thing they professed to be preserving.

On May 15, 1865, after the close of hostilities, Major Reilly took the oath of allegiance to the United States at Fort Delaware and was released. Union official records describe his appearance at the time as, "ruddy complexion, hair mixed, eyes blue and 5' 8" tall." Major Reilly anxiously returned home to his family and friends in Wilmington, North Carolina to begin his new civilian life.

While a prisoner at Chesapeake Hospital under the care of Union physicians,

Colonel Lamb also received a surprise visitor. Union General Curtis, also badly wounded and unable to walk, learned that his adversary from Fort Fisher was a patient at the same hospital. He ordered two hospital attendants to take him to Colonel Lamb's room. Curtis warmly greeted Lamb and congratulated him on his superb defense, fortitude, and bravery at Fort Fisher. When Curtis said, "I am proud of you as an American," Lamb responded, "I'm not an American – I'm a Confederate." General Curtis replied, "We will not discuss that subject. Your side or mine will control this country. It will not be divided. You and I will be in it and I offer you my hand and friendship. Let it begin now, not years later." The two men shook hands. For the next forty-four years, Colonel Lamb and General Curtis maintained a close friendship, working together to help heal the wounds between the North and the South. The minie ball that wounded Colonel Lamb's hip and leg at Fort Fisher was not extracted for nine months and he walked on crutches for seven years after the war.

General Whiting's health continued to fail from the effects of his wounds and dysentery. He died at Fort Columbus on Friday, March 10, 1865. Only days before his death, General Benjamin Butler, "The Yankee Beast," sent one of his staff officers to take an oral deposition from General Whiting. Butler hoped Whiting's testimony would help vindicate him from his failed December 1864 attack on Fort Fisher, which was being investigated by the Congressional Committee on the Conduct of the War.

Questioning General Whiting helped to seal Butler's reputation as an inconsiderate and arrogant opportunist. Butler's aide asked Whiting twenty-four questions concerning the powder vessel, the naval bombardment and the land attack on Fort Fisher. A typical question asked, "How near did the powder boat which exploded come to Fort Fisher?" Whiting answered, "Between twelve hundred and fifteen hundred yards, not nearer." Reinforcing his already poor reputation, Butler's decision to question his dying opponent did nothing to help his cause.

After succumbing to his wounds, General Whiting was buried in New York. On March 13, 1865, The *New York Daily News* printed the following obituary:

One of the most prominent matters in which Christian civilization differs from that which obtained under the rule of paganism is the administration of the rights of sepulcre to the remains of a deceased enemy.

The superiority of the former over the latter was very noticeable on the occasion of the obsequies, on Saturday, at Trinity Church, of the late Major-General W. H. C. Whit-

ing who was wounded at the taking of Fort Fisher, being in command of that garrison, transferred, on his arrival here, to Governor's Island, as a prisoner of war, and who died of his wounds in the military hospital there on Friday last.

A very large concourse of people was present, and the profoundest respect was paid to the deceased and his sorrowing relatives and friends. General Beall (the agent in this city for supplying the Confederacy with soldier's blankets in exchange for cotton) with five other intimate friends of the deceased General, most of whom are paroled Confederate officers, acted as pall-bearers on the occasion. Several Federal officers, in uniform, were in attendance at the obsequies.

The pall-bearers were Gen. Beall, of the Confederate service and General Stone, Major Trowbridge, Major Prime and Lt. Mowry, of the United States Service, and Mr. S. L. Merchant-C.B.D. The Rev. Dr. Morgan Dix, rector of Trinity, was the officiating minister, assisted by Rev. Dr. Ogilvie.

The corpse of the deceased was brought from Governor's Island about 12:30 o'clock Saturday morning and placed in the vestibule of The Trinity, where for half an hour the friends and relatives were allowed to view the features of the late general.

The body was embalmed, and on the coffin lid were laid beautiful floral offerings of natural camellias, in the shape of a cross and a heart. The face of the deceased was of the handsomest and most manly character. The coffin was rosewood, silver-mounted, and the breastplate bore the following inscription

Major-General W. H.C. Whiting, CSA
Born in the state of Mississippi
Died on Governor's Island, New York Harbor
March 10, 1865
Age 40 years, 11 months and 18 days

After it had been closed, lady friends of the deceased placed upon the lid two beautiful crosses of white camellias, fringed with evergreen, and a wreath of the same.

Shortly after 1 o'clock, Drs. Dix and Ogilvie began the solemn service in accordance with the prescribed ritual of the Episcopal Church. The coffin was then placed in front of the altar, and as it was borne up the aisle, an incident that attracted some attention was *the placing upon the coffin, by a young lady, a beautiful cluster of camellias, bound with black ribbon.*

After the usual services, the prayer of the commitment was read by Dr. Dix, at the foot of the coffin.

After the benediction, the body was borne to the waiting hearse, and the solemn cortege of carriages passed down Broadway en route to Greenwood, where his remains were placed in a receiving vault.

Ironically, General Whiting's brother, Robert Whiting, was the caretaker of Greenwood Cemetery, and was in charge of burying his brother. Thirty-five years later, on June 19, 1900, Mrs. Katherine Davis Walker Whiting, the general's wife, had her husband's body removed and re-interred in Oakdale Cemetery in Wilmington, North Carolina. Mrs. Whiting dressed in black mourning clothing most of the remainder of her life and never remarried. She died on November 21, 1901 and was buried beside her husband in Oakdale Cemetery. General Whiting's sister, Cecilia, a nun of the Sisterhood of the Good Shepherd in New York, died there in 1894. She is buried at Oakdale Cemetery behind the Whitings. A simple white cross marks her grave.

CHAPTER X

LEE'S WITHDRAWAL AND THE RESUMPTION OF PEACE

In the trenches of Petersburg the men were starving, and no food, clothing or military supplies were forthcoming. Shortages of copper caused an acute lack of percussion caps. This hopeless situation led to a high rate of desertion. On January 15, 1865, the fall of Fort Fisher closed the port of Wilmington, North Carolina, the last major Confederate port open to blockade runners, dealing a fatal blow to Lee's supply line. The Union's "Anaconda" had tightened its final coil around the Confederacy.

On February 1, 1865, Captain John Andrew Ramsay received a thirty day furlough because of a recurrence of his previous medical conditions. He returned home to Salisbury, North Carolina, where he remained until the end of hostilities. First Lieutenant Jesse F. Woodard, one of the original elected officers and a resident of Wayne County, North Carolina, commanded the battery until its surrender at Appomattox, Virginia.

In late March, General Lee planned a surprise attack against Fort Stedman on the Petersburg line to be led by Major General John B. Gordon. He hoped this last serious attempt to break the siege would open a way for the Army of Northern Virginia to reach the Confederate army in North Carolina, commanded by Lieutenant General Joe Johnston. The attack began at four in the morning on March 25 and completely surprised the Union defenders. By eight that morning, however, the Federals successfully counterattacked and recaptured Fort Stedman.

General Lee was trapped in his own lines with no hope of breaking out without abandoning Richmond. Sensing Lee's vulnerable situation, General Grant sent a large Union force under General Philip Sheridan to attack Lee's far southern right flank at Five Forks on April 1. Sheridan's attack sent the Confederates reeling and resulted in the capture of approximately four thousand five hundred troops.

On Sunday, April 2, General Lee sent a courier to President Davis, informing him that the line had broken and advising him that Richmond should be evacuated. Davis received the message while attending services at St. Paul's Church in Richmond and immediately ordered the capital's evacuation. The Confederate government and the entire city were thrown into chaos. That evening retreating Confederates torched much of Richmond, destroying arsenals and the fleet anchored in the James River. Federal occupation forces entered the city the following day. General Lee and the Army of Northern Virginia retreated to the southwest.

General E. P. Alexander promptly moved his five-mile long artillery train of wagons, field guns, siege guns and mortars out of the doomed Richmond and Petersburg area. The artillery made its way to a predetermined meeting place at Amelia Court House to rejoin General Lee and the rest of the Army of Northern Virginia. The roads leading west from Richmond were clogged with retreating Confederate troops, wagon trains and refugees, fleeing the advancing Union cavalry.

Ramsay's Battery, commanded during the retreat by Lieutenant Jesse F. Woodard, consisted of four to five "New Armstrong" British guns. In addition to Ramsay's Battery, Haskell's battalion included Lamkin's, Flanner's, and Garden's batteries. Captain James Nelson Lamkin from Nelson County, Virginia commanded a battery of large iron siege mortars. When the Petersburg line collapsed, Haskell moved his battalion from the Fort Harrison area. Attached to General Ewell's wagon train column, they crossed the Mayo Bridge over the James River and followed the Manchester Turnpike west. Captain Lamkin's eight or ten huge iron mortars were mounted on wagons, dragged by straining horses and prodded on by whip-wielding teamsters. Cannoneers, traditionally unarmed, walked alongside their wagons without swords or muskets.

Continuing their march westward, the column traveled through Old Coalfield, Virginia and took the Buckingham Road. Ewell's wagon train and Haskell's battalion passed through Powhatan Court House, Macon, Bellona, and Ballsville, before turning south at Tobaccoville and crossing the Appomattox River on the Clementown Bridge. The column then followed the Painesville Road across Flat Creek during the early morning hours of Wednesday, April 5.

A slow drizzle that began this gray day soon turned into a downpour. The column entered Amelia County and approached Flat Creek Swamp. At Paines Cross Roads, a horseman dressed in a Confederate officer's uniform directed the wagon train toward Painesville. Following his directions, they soon found themselves in a Yankee trap. The officer was a Union scout in disguise, nineteen year old J.A. Campbell. Campbell served under General Sheridan, who called him "Boy." As the trap sprung, several hundred Union cavalrymen surprised Haskell's battalion and the rest of the column. They charged through the deep swamp and dashed among the Confederate wagons in an instant. Ramsay's Battery was able to place one gun in firing position, but the charging Federal cavalry was too fast for them and captured all of the British Armstrong guns along with ninety-eight men and the battery's battle flag. Only Lieutenant Woodard and twenty-eight of his men eluded capture.

The attacking Union cavalry, commanded by Brigadier General Henry E. Davies, Jr., consisted of the First Pennsylvania, the First New Jersey and the Twenty-Fourth New York. They captured four to five guns from Ramsay's Batttery, plus eleven battle flags, three hundred and twenty white soldiers, four hundred colored teamsters and over four hundred animals from other units, all of which they took to Jetersville, Virginia. The Yankees burned over two hundred Confederate wagons, including caissons, ambulances and ammunition wagons. They also burned headquarters wagons, most likely including General E. P. Alexander's personal wagon. The personal wagons of Generals Custis Lee and Fitzhugh Lee were also set ablaze later that day. Marching some distance behind the column, the First Regiment of Engineers soon came upon the scene. They found many undestroyed wagons, containing sugar, beans, flour, and medical supplies. They also found kegs of whiskey that had burst open. The whiskey ran out of the kegs and collected in the holes and wheel tracks on the dirt road. The resourceful engineers licked up the whiskey, mud and all. They then filled their haversacks with food and moved on to Deatonville.

At first sight of the charging Yankees, the brave and loyal Captain Lamkin, a gigantic Confederate officer crippled with rheumatism, gave his horse to a courier with instructions to deliver vital and important maps to General Alexander. He was promptly captured by the charging Federal cavalry.

Lieutenant Woodard and the remainder of Ramsay's Battery, along with other cannoneers, followed Colonel Haskell towards Amelia Court House for badly needed rations. Rail cars containing food had been burned in Richmond. The retreat continued to Rice's Station on April 6. Pursued by Union cavalry, the Army of Northern Virginia could not stop to rest.

On April 7, the remnants of the army pushed on through High Bridge toward Farmville, where rations had been found for the starving troops. By April 8, the artillery column neared Appomattox Court House. There, the remaining portion of Ramsay's Battery took a defensive position early on the morning of April 9. They engaged in a short skirmish with the pursuing Federals, most likely on foot as "red leg infantry," since their guns had been captured. Sometime before noon word reached the men on both sides that General Lee had initiated communications with General Grant to surrender the Army of Northern Virginia and bring about "the resumption of peace."

The surrender took place in the front parlor of the Wilmer McLean house between one and four in the afternoon on Palm Sunday, April 9, 1865. General Lee dressed in a striking new uniform described as "a snowy linen material." He wore a magnificent dress sword with the inscription, "Aide-toi et dien t'aidera," meaning "Help yourself and God will help you."

The formal stacking of arms took place on April 12. After four long years of fighting, the war was over. Tears were plentiful during this extremely emotional time. The Confederate troops would have another burden to bear when they returned home. Many would find devastation and financial ruin. The gallant men of the Rowan Artillery gave their all for the cause of Southern freedom. They made their way back to North Carolina to start new lives, facing Federal occupation and Reconstruction.

Shortly before the war began in the spring of 1861, Union General Winfield Scott summed up his feeling toward the seceding southern states when he wrote, "Wayward sisters, depart in peace." Many observers at that time and since have expressed the opinion that the southern states would have found their way back into the Union without war earlier than they did with war. While the benefits and detriments of an independent South or a Union preserved by force continue to be debated, the hard facts remain clear. For four long years, the history of the nation was written in the blood of approximately six hundred and thirty thousand men killed and over one million wounded.

When the Confederate artillery surrendered, only sixty-one field pieces remained out of two hundred and fifty in service when they left Richmond. Thirteen caissons and a total of two thousand five hundred and eighty-six artillerymen surrendered at Appomattox. Colonel Haskell's battalion had been whittled down to fifteen officers and one hundred and thirty-nine enlisted men. Ramsay's Battery, commanded by Lieutenant Woodard, had less than thirty men and officers and no guns.

Colonel Haskell supervised handing over the Army of Northern Virginia's guns to the Federals. He worked with Union Brevet Major General Joseph J. Bartlett of the First Division, Fifth Corps. After working together for several days, completing and signing forms and receipts, the two men formed a bond. Haskell sold Bartlett one of his beautiful horses, since Confederate officers were only allowed to take one horse home along with their side arms. Haskell always had exceptionally fast and beautiful horses, a fact that impressed noted animal lover, General Lee. Haskell later sent a set of English "horse clothing" and a bridle to Bartlett at his home in New York, but the two men never saw each other again.

Colonel John C. Haskell had been engaged on February 29, 1864 to the beautiful Miss Sarah "Sally" Hampton, daughter of the famous cavalry commander, General Wade Hampton. They were married June 21, 1865. Colonel Haskell moved to Mississippi to operate a plantation, but after a few years returned to Columbia, South Carolina to practice law. Haskell was greatly saddened by Sally's death, April 7, 1886. A few years later he married Sally's cousin, Lucy Hampton. Colonel Haskell was elected to the South Carolina legislature in 1877 and again in 1890. He died on June 26, 1906 and was buried in the old graveyard at Trinity Episcopal Church in downtown Columbia.

During General Lee's retreat toward Appomattox, Colonel Haskell witnessed an interesting incident between Lieutenant General James Longstreet and Major General George A. Custer of the Yankee cavalry, which he described as follows

A Union officer came dashing up to Maj. Gibbes. He was a most striking picture: a rather young man, dressed in a blue sack coat with the largest shoulder-straps of a major general I ever saw; with long red hair hanging in oily curls down near to his shoulders, a gorgeous red scarf in which there was a gold pin, nearly two inches in length and breadth, with big letters, 'George A. Custer, Major General.'

As Custer swaggered up to Longstreet, he called out so loud that all around must hear, 'I have come to demand your instant surrender. We are in a position to crush you and unless you surrender at once we will destroy you.' Longstreet said: 'By what authority do you come into our lines? General Lee is in communication with General Grant. We certainly will not recognize any subordinate.'

Custer immediately swaggered out, 'Oh Sheridan and I are independent of Grant and we will destroy you if you don't surrender at once.' Longstreet answered: 'I suppose you know no better and have violated the decencies of military procedure because you know no better. But your ignorance will not save you if you do so again. Now go, and act as you and Sheridan choose; and I will teach you a lesson you won't forget.' Then raising his voice and shaking his finger, he repeated, 'Now go.'

If I ever saw a man with his tail between his legs, it was Custer. He asked for safe-guard back to his own lines, and someone pointed to Colonel Osmun Latrobe, Longstreet's adjutant general. Custer came up to and asked him for a guard. It appeared that when he came into our lines with a handkerchief in his hand, some of our men pulled him off and handled him rather roughly, though they did not injure him. He saw Major Gibbes, with whom he had been at West Point, and made a most clamorous appeal for protection. It was in this way that Gibbes had happened to bring him to Longstreet.

Custer was mounted on a very inferior horse and when Latrobe gave him a guard, he saw some very handsome horses standing there. At once recovering his self-possession, he expressed a desire for one that happened to be mine. I told him it was not for sale or plunder, and asked him to tell us if Colonel Frank Huger was living, as I noticed that he was wearing Colonel Huger's spurs. They were a very handsome pair of gold-mounted, Mexican spurs, which Santa Ana had worn during the Mexican War and which were given to General Huger, Colonel Frank's father, who was chief of ordnance on Scott's staff. Custer flushed, and said that he had only taken them to care for them for Huger, who had been his friend at West Point. Years after, Colonel Huger told me that he had never been able to get them from Custer, who insisted on continuing to take care of them until his death.

Incidents such as this were perceived as examples of the "Yankee way of preserving the Union." Colonel Frank Huger after the war held several high positions in the southern railroad industry. He died on July 10, 1897 in Roanoke, Virginia, at the age of sixty.

General Henry J. Hunt, the great Union artillery commander, was present for the surrender at Appomattox Court House. Remaining there for a few days afterwards, he renewed old friendships from the Mexican War, including Generals Longstreet, Wilcox, and Lee. He also met his Confederate counterpart, General W. N. Pendleton. Hunt was surprised to find General A. L. Long, his artillery pupil from the old Fort Washita days, not in good health or emotional condition. Hunt spent over an hour trying to cheer up Long. General Long remarked to his old artillery instructor that he was sorry for the poor showing of the Confederate artillery on the third day at Gettysburg and always wondered how Hunt reacted to that performance.

General Long then defended the Confederate artillery's capabilities during the retreat from Gettysburg. He told Hunt that on July 14, 1863, near Williamsport, Maryland the Army of the Potomac would "have been thumped" if they had attacked the Confederates' superior artillery position.

Hunt lingered a little longer, reminiscing, and then returned to his camp. The great artillery duels between the armies were now in the past and would become the subject of war stories told by graying veterans to their children and grandchildren.

CHAPTER XI

THE PATRIOT'S HEART

When General Lee surrendered the Army of Northern Virginia at Appomattox Court House, Captain Ramsay remained on medical leave in Salisbury, North Carolina. On April 12, only three days after Lee's surrender, Union General George Stoneman, with four thousand troops, rushed into Salisbury to free Union prisoners held at the Confederate prison camp. Angered to find that five hundred Union prisoners had been moved to Charlotte, leaving behind only those who were too weak or lame to walk, Stoneman decided to destroy everything useful in the town, insuring that the citizens would not wish to continue fighting. He burned all public buildings with the exception of the court house. Stoneman had eaten breakfast at the home of T. J. Meroney and was so pleased with the courteous treatment he received there that he granted Mr. Meroney his wish that the Federal troops spare the Rowan County Court House.

A forty-two year old New York native, General Stoneman had graduated in 1846 from West Point, where his roommate was Stonewall Jackson. After the war he moved to California, where he served as governor from 1883 to 1887. Stoneman's raid on Salisbury was memorialized by Robbie Robertson's 1969 rock and roll song, *The Night They Drove Old Dixie Down*.

Salisbury contained a sizeable cache of Confederate stores. Stoneman captured eighteen guns, ten thousand stands of arms, a hundred and sixty thousand pounds of bacon, seven thousand bales of cotton, two hundred and fifty thousand blankets and thousands of Confederate uniforms, highlighting that the shortages suffered by the armies resulted from poor communication and distribution. Stoneman's troops raided downtown stores and hauled their goods to a pile in the street across from the court house. Yankee soldiers took what they wanted and gave some to blacks and poor whites, who came begging. Then they set the remainder on fire.

The following excerpts from the personal recollections of Margaret Ellen

Beall Ramsay, widow of John Ramsay's cousin, provide an eyewitness account of Stoneman's raid:

All night long, at intervals, the muffled roar of cannonading at the Yadkin River Bridge miles away was heard with a shudder. No one can conceive of that night's terror. Morning finally came. At last the sun rose, but as it's beams struggled through the morning mist, they brought little ease to our broken spirits. After eating a hasty breakfast, I gathered my small children about me, went to my bedroom on the second story, sat down at a front window and was watching and waiting breathlessly when the storm of Stoneman's cavalry, numbering 4,000, swooped down upon us. The missiles were flying fit and fast around and upon the house. Then plunging their horses over the fence, some of soldiers rushed into the hall and up the steps, demanding of me, "The damned rebel who lives here."

Downstairs the men were ransacking, pillaging, wielding their swords among the terrified servants and shouting, 'Make me some coffee! Fry me some meat! Make me some bread or I'll cut you in two!' I was horrified to see Judge Caldwell, old and feeble, dragged by the ruffians into his yard while they wielded their swords above his head, demanding his valuables. They threatened to hang him but on consideration of his age, let him go. At the same time, his wagon of provisions and valuables was captured in front of my door. All through the day the soldiers were in and out of my home. When an officer spied my piano, he asked me to play a tune. I replied, 'I cannot play. There is no music in my soul today.' I took my children and fled to my sister Lizzie's home in another part of the county. While there I received a message from the soldiers in my home to return for they didn't mean to frighten me away. When I did return I found they had filled my pantry with a large supply of food before moving on.

Margaret Ramsay, a young and attractive widow with small children, must have struck a note of kindness and compassion in the hearts of these Union men.

By May 1865, with North Carolina's government under Union control, Provisional Governor W. W. Holden, a Yankee sympathizer and "scalawag" politician, appointed John Ramsay chief of police of the Town of Salisbury. Ramsay held this position during the early days of Union occupation and reconstruction.

While serving in the army, Captain John A. Ramsay frequently corresponded with his cousin, Julius David Ramsay of Salisbury, who looked after his personal business. On June 19, 1864, Julius died at the age of thirty-eight, leaving his wife, Margaret Ellen Beall Ramsay, to care for their two children, William and

184

Minnie. While on medical leave from the Army of Northern Virginia, John A. Ramsay likely visited his cousin's widow and comforted her during her period of mourning.

On June 19, 1865, Captain Ramsay took the Federal Oath of Allegiance and was officially paroled at Salisbury. Confederates referred to taking the Union oath as "swallowing the dog." After a short courtship and "viewing the comet," Captain Ramsay proposed marriage to Margaret. Reverend Jethro Rumple married them at the First Presbyterian Church of Salisbury on July 26, 1865. Margaret was twenty-four and John was twenty-eight. They were married for more than forty years, when John died in 1909.

The couple moved into a small house at 425 South Fulton Street in Salisbury. John Ramsay again took up surveying and engineering as his primary profession. His outstanding accomplishments included laying out one of the town's first sewer systems and supervising a gang of workers as Superintendent of Streets. He also designed the original building for the Frank B. John School on Ellis Street, which still stands and serves as the administration offices for the Rowan County School System. Politically, Ramsay joined the moderate wing of the Republican Party, which attempted to reconcile northern efforts at reconstruction with the restoration of political rights to former Confederates. These moderates chose Captain Ramsay to head their ticket in the mayoral race, which he won in 1879 and again in 1880. He was not reelected in 1881.

While serving as mayor in 1879, Ramsay led a successful movement to tax property owners to help build and support public schools. The school on Ellis Street was paid for with money from this new tax revenue system. Ramsay ran for mayor again in 1883 and won. During this term he worked hard to promote education for the poor. He was defeated in the election of 1884 and retired from local politics until 1896, when he was elected to one term as North Carolina state senator from the district composed of Cabarrus, Rowan and Forsyth Counties. After his legislative term, Ramsay returned to his surveying and engineering business. A devout Presbyterian, he taught Sunday school and served for many years as an elder at the First Presbyterian Church of Salisbury. He was also a pioneer member and officer of the State Sunday School. On the lighter side, he played the tuba in the Salisbury Brass Band.

An undated account describes Captain Ramsay presenting his personal recollections of General Lee and the Battle of Sharpsburg at the invitation of the Robert Hoke Chapter of the United Daughters of the Confederacy. "With a voice filled with emotion," this account relates, "his locks silvered and the courage born in a patriot's heart illuminating his brow, there was not an eye that did not weep as he told of the valiant braves who fought to save the storm cradled nation that fell. He told of his close association with General Lee and their many conversations, of the love of his army and the respect the Federal troops evinced."

Like so many other veterans, Ramsay was entitled to receive a pension from the state of North Carolina. Many veterans gathered at the Davis & Wiley Bank in Salisbury to cash their pension checks. There, curious citizens often confronted them, asking them in which regiments and batteries and under what officers they had served.

On one particular occasion, a young onlooker teased an old veteran of Ramsay's Battery by inquiring, "Captain Ramsay was scared most of the time, wasn't he?" The old veteran replied, "Who? Him? Captain John Ramsay? Why, man, he wasn't scared of nothin' or nobody. I've seen him lead his men into battle, and I was one of them, and it was never 'go,' but 'come on, men,' and if anyone was looking for somebody who was scared, he needn't fool away any time with Captain Ramsay." He then added that one day he observed Ramsay after a skirmish with the Federals, sitting on a log reading a dispatch that was just handed to him, when a Yankee bullet knocked it out of his hand. The legend is that he reached down and picked it up as calmly as if only a gust of wind had taken it away.

Out of love for the artillery and feelings of nostalgia for the Lost Cause, Captain Ramsay purchased an old wrought iron cannon from a Salisbury foundryman named Marsh. This cannon, dating from the period of the War Between the States, was probably used to guard the Salisbury Confederate prison camp. The tube measured fifty inches long with a three and three quarter inch smooth bore. It assumed an active role in Salisbury's community life, when it was placed in Ramsay's back yard, facing Monroe Street, on a makeshift carriage. This cannon was only fired on special occasions, first when the train returning President Jefferson Davis's body to Richmond came through Salisbury. The Ramsay cannon could also be heard every Fourth of July, as well as for the annual Guilford Battleground Celebration. Once early in the morning of July 26, 1876, a group of mischievous boys fired the old cannon, waking the entire neighborhood.

A family tradition relates that Captain Ramsay put his son, John Ernest Ramsay, in charge of firing the cannon to salute President Theodore Roosevelt's train, when it arrived in Salisbury. The train was late, and Captain Ramsay finally told his son to begin firing the cannon because he could hear the train coming. John Ernest Ramsay later recalled, "I heard a train, and we started firing salutes. Suddenly a horseman came dashing up to the cannon. 'Cease fire,' he shouted, 'that's a freight train!'"

The cannon also fired on November 11, 1918, to commemorate Armistice Day, and returned to service in 1945 to celebrate the signing of the Japanese surrender ending World War II. Today, the old out-of-service Captain Ramsay cannon can be seen at the beautiful Dr. Josephus W. Hall home on Jackson Street, the home of the Historic Salisbury Foundation.

After several weeks of illness and a rapid decline, Captain John A. Ramsay passed away on January 27, 1909 at his home in Salisbury at the age of seventy-two. He left behind his wife, Margaret, and two sons, Dr. R. L. Ramsay and John E. Ramsay, all residents of Salisbury. The Captain's funeral took place at the First Presbyterian Church at four in the afternoon on January 28 with pastor, Dr. Byron Clarke, presiding. Graveside services were held at Chestnut Hill Cemetery in Salisbury. This brave and gallant Confederate cavalier, who served St. Barbara, the patron saint of artillery, so well, was then put to rest. His soul was escorted by a gathering of angels into the Kingdom of the Lord. Blessed is this man of God that the Yankees could not kill.

The United Daughters of the Confederacy and the Confederate Veterans Association erected a monument at the intersection of Dock Street and Third Street in downtown Wilmington, North Carolina in 1924 to honor the city's Confederate veterans. The monument was designed by noted architect Henry Bacon, Jr., who had also designed the Lincoln Memorial in Washington, D.C. Bacon, who grew up mostly in coastal North Carolina, considered Wilmington his home. He is buried in Oakdale Cemetery in Wilmington.

Captain John A. Ramsay's son, John, had the honor to be chosen as the model for this bronze sculpture. John Ernest Ramsay worked as manager for the Harris Granite Company of Salisbury, and the sculptor, F. H. Packer, met him while selecting granite for the base of the monument. The sculptor thought that John Ernest Ramsay's face and features symbolized the nobility of the men who fought for the South.

CHAPTER XII

A GOOD OLE IRISH REBEL

Returning to his home and family in Wilmington, North Carolina in May 1865, Major Reilly accepted a position as superintendent of the Wilmington and Brunswick Ferry Company. The ferry crossed the Cape Fear River between Wilmington and Eagle Island. In 1874 the Reilly family purchased a Greek Revival style house at 111 South Sixth Street in Wilmington, where they resided until 1883.

Major Reilly's wife, Ann Quinn Reilly, died on July 20, 1877 at the age of forty-seven. The Reillys had one son and three daughters, who reached maturity. One daughter, Katherine Whiting Reilly Donlan, was named after the wife of General W. H. C. Whiting, reflecting the long and close friendship between the men and their families. Major Reilly married Miss Martha E. Henry on September 20, 1878 at the home of her father, William R. Henry, of Columbus County, North Carolina. The Reverend Father Moore conducted the ceremonies. The major and Martha had two daughters, Madge and Anna Jane. Martha Henry Reilly was born on April 25, 1841 and died December 27, 1919. She is buried next to Major Reilly at Oakdale Cemetery in Wilmington.

The *Wilmington Star* contains a number of interesting articles, chronicling Major Reilly's post war activities. A sampling of these articles read:

A MYSTERIOUS AFFAIR, September 30, 1868

> *It was reported in our city yesterday, by Mr. Israel Thomas, of Brunswick County, that a mule and buggy were found by a negro on Monday night in a lonely place on the Brunswick Road, ten or twelve miles from this place. The mule was detached from the buggy, and the harness broken. In the buggy, an overcoat, a carpet-bag containing a quantity of clothes, and a number of salted fish were found. The negro brought the mule and conveyance to the city.*

As this spot is quite an out-of-the-way place, a suspicion of some foul play is natu-
rally created. Maj. Reilly, at the ferry here, recollects a white man crossing in this buggy
and with the same mule, about three weeks ago, bound, it is thought, on a peddling tour
along the coast. It may have been thought that he had about his person quite a sum of
money, for which he may have been murdered. The affair is yet in doubt. It may, perhaps,
be cleared up in a few days, either by confirmation of suspicions or the discovery of the
missing man.

MAY 23, 1869

Mr. James Reilly, ferry keeper, is my agent in Wilmington for the sales of shingles.
Persons in want of shingles for building purposes, or for shipment, will please call on him
at the Ferry, where samples can be seen.

(signed) H. B. Short

On April 8, 1876, Major Reilly received by mail a Mexican War medal that
was prepared by the National Association of Veterans of the Mexican War to
honor Reilly's service during that conflict. The *Wilmington Star* described the medal
as follows:

A modified American shield, the outer rim raised from the general surface, and
having thereon the names of battles of the Mexican War. Left upper corner: a man-
of-war, navy. Apex of center: a bursting bomb, ordnance. Central group of arms:
rifle, volunteer element; musket, saber and pistol, infantry and cavalry. Right upper
corner: a field piece, artillery. Directly under group of arms the word 'Mexico' in black.
Thereunder a maguey plant surrounded by cactus, emblematic of Mexico. Thereunder
a castle: engineers. Thereunder the figures '1846,' date of war. The four last are sur-
rounded by laurel wreath. Surrounding the wreath, twenty-nine five-pointed stars:
number of states at date of war.

By June 1882, Major Reilly resigned his position with the Wilmington and
Brunswick Ferry Company, which had passed into the hands of a new lessee, M.
H. Rouse. Reilly decided to retire to his plantation home, located at Farmer's
Turnout in Brunswick County, about eighteen miles west of Wilmington. Here
he became a productive farmer. He and his wife, Martha, both devout Catholics,
traveled to Wilmington to attend mass, since there was no Catholic church closer

to their home.

An article in *Our Lady of the Snow Parish Bulletin* for February and March 1954, describes Reilly's work to establish Saint Paul the Apostle Church at Farmer's Turnout. Around 1880 Major Reilly donated land to build a Catholic church at Farmer's Turnout. A recent convert, Lloyd McCoy, supplied the lumber for the new church and provided extra materials to build a church for the local black community. With labor donated by William R. Henry and his son-in-law, William Alderman, Charley Morrell oversaw construction. William Raphael Henry built the communion rails, interior walls and frames for the Stations of the Cross. Saint Paul the Apostle Church was dedicated by Bishop H. P. Northrop of Charleston in 1882, with Father Marck serving as the parish priest. A large crowd celebrated the dedication, including many who arrived on a special train, which left Wilmington's Front Street at nine in the morning and returned at three thirty in the afternoon. Tickets cost seventy-five cents for adults and fifty cents for children. Mass was said once a month until 1902. During this time, Father Christopher Dennen, Father Patrick Moore, Fathers Burns, Schall, Driffin, O'Brien and Marion came from Wilmington to serve the parishioners.

As the founding leaders of the Catholic families died and their descendants left the area, the church was abandoned and stood in disrepair for many years. An attempt to re-establish Saint Paul the Apostle Church began in 1929, but was unsuccessful because there were not enough families in the area to support a church. Once again it fell into disrepair and was dismantled, its parts used in the construction of other nearby Catholic churches, including St. Francis Xavier Church in Tabor City and Sacred Heart Church in Southport.

Next to the church, land was designated for a cemetery. Many residents of the area were buried there, including members of the Henry, Alderman, Williams, Herring and Twiggs families.

In 1888 Major Reilly and other Catholics in the vicinity of Farmer's Turnout decided to build a school. The Catholic school, like the church, suffered from low attendance and lack of financial support and closed after only seven years.

Saturday, February 25, 1888, saw President Grover Cleveland and Mrs. Cleveland visiting Farmer's Turnout in North Carolina. Major Reilly knew that President Cleveland was on a political tour and planned to stop at South Island, just outside Georgetown, South Carolina, to visit his old friend, General E. Porter Alexander, Reilly's First Corps artillery commander in the Army of Northern Virginia. The president intended to go duck hunting on General Alexander's hunting preserve, which today is known as the Yawkey Wildlife Preserve, managed by Bob

Joyner. General Alexander also owned a summer cottage, "The Wigwam," at Flat Rock, North Carolina, where he played golf with many of his wartime cronies. "The Wigwam" has changed very little over the years, and today the Dunn family owns the building and the surrounding property.

Major Reilly supplied the railroad trains passing through Farmer's Turnout with wood to fuel their steam engines. Making use of this connection, he arranged for President Cleveland's train to make a ten minute or more stop at Farmer's Turnout. The residents placed a large arch of holly and cedar over the track, bearing the words, "Our Honored President is Welcomed to North Carolina." Major Reilly presided over the occasion, and after shaking hands with the president, introduced him to the crowd. Then Reilly escorted Cleveland to Saint Paul's School so that he could say a few words to the children and their teacher, Miss Elizabeth Darby. The president's wife, Frances Folsom Cleveland, a remarkably handsome woman, made a very pleasant impression. She was beautifully attired in a garnet cashmere dress, trimmed with braid, complimented by a corsage of pink hyacinths. Their rail car contained many tropical fruits and bouquets of beautiful flowers, which had been presented to them along the route from Florida.

The *Wilmington Morning Star News* continued to chronicle many of Major Reilly's activities. In December 1891, the paper reported that Reilly had visited the city and renewed his subscription to the *Star*. Referring to the civil war then raging in Chile, the paper commented that when Reilly was "asked if he would not like to step down to South America and fight Chile, he said no; but if they would come near Wilmington, he might 'take a hand'."

In June 1893, articles quoted below from the *Morning Star News* described Colonel William Lamb's visit to Wilmington and Fort Fisher:

Col. Lamb and his family came to Wilmington at the invitation of Cape Fear Camp No. 254 United Confederate Veterans. They were met at the railway station by the veterans and escorted to the Orton Plantation. The next day Major James Reilly as part of a committee went with Col. Lamb by steamer down the Cape Fear River to visit Fort Fisher. During the two hour boat trip there were many remembrances and conversations about the fort. After arriving at the rocks and having dinner "lunch" at a restaurant built upon the ruins of Battery Buchanan the group toured what was left of old Fort Fisher.

That evening Col. Lamb gave an excellent lecture on Fort Fisher at the Y.M.C.A. in Wilmington. On the platform with Col. Lamb were Maj. James Reilly hero of Fort

Fisher, Col. William L. DeRosset, Mr. James C. Stevenson and Col. Alfred M. Waddell. Col. Lamb complimented the brave and gallant Maj. Reilly for his efforts in trying to save Fort Fisher from the invading Yankee fleet. The audience went wild with cheering and applause for their local hero Maj. James Reilly.

On July 7, 1893, the *Morning Star* reported on the Major's agricultural accomplishments in the following article:

Maj. James Reilly, of Brunswick, has left at the Star office a sample of his oat crop, grown on sandy land, which is a wonder. The stalks are nearly six feet in height, are well headed, and are only an average sample of the whole crop. As a transformer of 'swords into ploughshares,' the Major has proved a success.

Also in 1893, as previously related, Major Reilly corresponded with former Union Captain E. Lewis Moore of Massachusetts, who returned the sword that Major Reilly had surrendered at Fort Fisher. The sword and its scabbard were produced by the Ames Manufacturing Company of Chicopee, Massachusetts in 1859. Marked "U.S. G.G.S." on the blade and "J.H. JWR" on the brass butt of the hilt, it was a light cavalry saber with a curved blade thirty-one and one half inches long and one half inch wide. During a reunion of the survivors of Fort Fisher a few years after his death, Major Reilly's sword was exhibited in the show window of C. W. Yates & Company on Market Street in Wilmington. The sword is presently on loan to the State of North Carolina and can be seen on display at the beautiful state historic site at Fort Fisher, where it was placed by Major Reilly's grandson, the late Lawrence Lee of Wilmington.

Widely known as an old veteran and a historical figure, Major Reilly lived out the remainder of his life at his plantation home at Farmer's Turnout. He earned a reputation as a good citizen, well liked by all who knew him. On November 6, 1894, the *Morning Star News* reported that he was very ill at his home, suffering from heart disease.

Major James Reilly passed away at ten o'clock Monday night, November 7, 1894 at the age of seventy-one. He left behind his second wife, Martha E. Henry Reilly, and their two daughters, Madge and Anna Jane, who resided with their mother. His children by his first wife, Ann Quinn Reilly, were Mrs. D. O'Connor of Wilmington, John W. Reilly, Superintendent of the Wilmington Gas & Light Company, Mrs. J. M. Donlon of Florence, South Carolina, and Mrs. J. Lockfaw of Wilmington. The next day Major Reilly's remains were sent to Wilmington on the Wilmington, Columbia and Augusta Railroad, arriving at eleven thirty in the morning. A number of Reilly's friends, as well as representatives of the Hibernian Society, met the train and escorted the coffin to the home of his son-in-law, Major D. O'Connor.

Captain John F. Divine, Colonel F. W. Kerchner, Colonel John L. Cantwell, Captain John Barry, E. S. Martin and F. Donlon served as pallbearers. The funeral took place at Major O'Connor's home on Princess Street, between Second and Front Streets. From there, the procession made its way to St. Thomas Catholic Church. Father Dennen conducted a solemn mass and paid a touching and fitting tribute to the life and character of Major Reilly. Numerous mourners, including the Cape Fear Camp of the United Confederate Veterans and the Hibernian Society, followed the hearse to Oakdale Cemetery. The many floral tributes required a special conveyance to the cemetery and the grave was covered with flowers. Major Reilly was buried next to his first wife. The second Mrs. Reilly was laid to rest next to the Major after her death in 1919.

Amazingly, during a lifetime of military service, Major Reilly was never seriously wounded. He took part in some of the fiercest and deadliest battles in American history, but his Irish luck and Catholic saints always protected him.

James Sprunt, a notable local historian, businessman and owner of the Orton Plantation on the Cape Fear River, sent the following letter of condolence to the Reilly family a few days after the funeral:

> *Being prevented at the last moment from attending the funeral services of my late dear friend, Maj. James Reilly, I desire to add my humble tribute to his memory, which I shall cherish as long as life lasts. I have known him intimately from my youth, and a braver, truer, kindlier man of our times has not, in my opinion, outlived him. Aside from his brilliant military record, which belongs to history, he had one of the warmest hearts, brimful of kindly and generous impulses, which through all the vicissitudes of life, sustained the affection of a wide circle of devoted friends. The close of his eventful career reminds one of the appropriate words of Marc Antony over the body of the dead Brutus, "His life was gentle and the elements so mixed in him, that nature might stand up and say to all the world, 'this was a man.'"*

On March 31, 1899, James Sprunt procured from Alexander Dickson & Sons of Belfast, Ireland some slips of roses and hawthorne taken from the fields near Athlone, the birthplace of Major Reilly, and carefully wrapped in Irish moss. At Sprunt's request, T. Donlon, the keeper of Oakdale Cemetery, reverently planted them on the grave of Mr. Sprunt's dead friend.

The following excerpts from a letter written about 1940 by Madge Reilly, Major Reilly's oldest daughter from his second marriage, to her niece, Annie Reilly Doerner, give a warm insight into Major Reilly's personality:

There are so many little things I remember hearing my father speak about, especially about Ireland. I was only 14 when he died, but I was with him so many hours and he taught me so many things. He used to make me memorize some of Thomas Moore's poems, make me read, write, copy letters, practice my music, and sing Civil War and Irish songs to me and so many other things. Do you remember when you were all little when he would go to your house, how all of you would meet him and he would hold 3 or 4 of you by the hand and march you up to the house.

A letter from Reilly's youngest daughter, Anna Jane, who was only thirteen when her father died, stated:

Major Reilly had to deal with a soldier who had been foraging for food, specifically trying to shoot a farmer's pig. Major Reilly told him how foolish he was by saying, "Bang goes the gun, squeal goes the pig, and into the guardhouse goes the fool."...I grew up in his shadow. He left me with a strict code of youthful conduct.

Anna Jane passed this code on to her own children with frequent reminders of what her father would, or would not, allow. He might have been a disciplinarian, but she remembered him as a loving and caring father and treasured many fond memories.

The soul of this "good ole" Irish Rebel soldier, Major James Reilly, was laid at the altar of St. Patrick. The angels will forever sing of his glorious deeds in the service of St. Barbara.

SOURCES

Alexander, Edward Porter, *Fighting For the Confederacy*. Edited by Gary W. Gallagher. Chapel Hill: University of North Carolina Press, 1989.

Almond, Barrie, *Crossfire: Journal of the ACWRT* (United Kingdom), No. 59, March 1999.

Baker, Gary R. *Cadets in Gray, The Story of the Cadets of the South Carolina Military Academy and the Cadet Rangers in the Civil War*. Columbia: Palmetto Bookworks, 1989.

Branch, Paul, "John A. Ramsay," biographical sketch in *Dictionary of North Carolina Biography*, edited by William S. Powell, volume 5. Chapel Hill: University of North Carolina Press, 1994.

Brock, R. A., ed. by, *Southern Historical Society Papers*, volume XXVI. Richmond, Va.: Southern Historical Society, 1898, 1909.

Brown, Kent Masterson, *Retreat From Gettysburg*. Chapel Hill: University of North Carolina Press, 2005.

Butler, Benjamin F., *Butler's Book, Autobiographical and Personal Reminiscences of Major-General Benj. F. Butler*. 2 volumes. Boston: A.M. Thayer & Co. Book Publishers, 1892.

The Carolina Watchman, May 1863.

Chesnut, Mary Boykin, *A Diary From Dixie.* Edited by Ben Ames Williams. Cambridge, Mass.: Harvard University Press, 1949.

Clark, Walter, ed., *Histories of the Several Regiments and Battalions From North Carolina in the Great War 1861-'65*. Reprint ed., Wendell, N.C.: Broadfoot's Bookmark, 1982.

Company Muster Rolls, North Carolina State Troops, North Carolina State Archives, Raleigh, North Carolina.

Confederate Service Records, National Archives, Washington, D.C.

Confederate Medical Director's Office, Hospital Records, National Archives, Washington, D.C.

Confederate Veteran, volume XX (1912).

Confederate Veteran, volume XI (1932).

Davis, William C., editor, *The Confederate General*, volume 4, Kelly, John to Payne, William H. Harrisburg, Pa.: National Historical Society, 1991.

Donnelly, Ralph W. *Biographical Sketches of the Commissioned Officers of the Confederate States Marine Corps*. Revised, expanded, and annotated by David M. Sullivan. Shippensburg, Pa.: White Mane Books, 1973.

Donnelly, Ralph W. *The Confederate States Marine Corps: The Rebel Leathernecks*. Shippensburg, Pa.: White Mane Publishing Co., 1989.

Eldredge, Capt. D. *The Third New Hampshire and All About It.* Boston: Press of E. B. Stillings and Company, 1893.

Evans, Clement, ed. *Confederate Military History,* volume V (North Carolina). Extended edition, Wilmington, N.C.: Broadfoot Publishing Company, 1987.

Evans, Eli, *Judah P. Benjamin: The Jewish Confederate.* N.Y.: The Free Press, 1988.

Farwell, Byron, *Stonewall, A Biography of General Thomas J. Jackson.* N.Y.: W. W. Norton & Company, 1992.

Fonvielle, Jr., Chris E. *The Wilmington Campaign, Last Rays of Departing Hope.* Campbell, California: Savas Publishing Co., 1987.

Fort Fisher Log Book, 1864. Fort Fisher State Historical Site, Wilmington, North Carolina.

Fort Washita Historic Site, website, http://www.ok-history.mus.ok.us/mussites/masnum09.htm.

Fremantle, Lt. Col. Arthur J. L., *Three Months in the Southern States.* Reprint edition, Lincoln: University of Nebraska Press, 1991.

Georgia Division, United Daughters of the Confederacy, *Confederate Reminiscences and Letters, 1861-1865.* Volume XIII, 2000.

Golay, Michael, *To Gettysburg and Beyond, The Parallel Lives of Joshua Lawrence Chamberlain and Edward Porter Alexander.* Shohocken, Pa.: Sarpedon Publishers, 2000.

Govan, Gilbert E. and James W. Livinggood, ed., *The Haskell Memoirs in His Own Words.* N.Y.: G. P. Putnam's Sons, 1960.

Gragg, Rod. *Confederate Goliath, The Battle of Fort Fisher.* New York: HarperCollins, 1991.

Harrison, Noel G., *State of Virginia Civil War Sites: Fredericksburg, December 1862-April 1865,* volume II. Lynchburg, Va.: H. E. Howard, 1995.

Hawkes, Charles, ed., *The Knapsack,* newsletter of the Raleigh Civil War Roundtable, Raleigh, N.C., volume 6, number 10 (October 2006).

Jackson, Harry L., *First Regiment Engineer Troops P.A.C.S., Robert E. Lee's Combat Engineers.* Louisa, Va.: R.A.E. Design and Publishing, 1998.

Johnson, Clint, *Bull's-Eyes and Misfires, 50 People Whose Obscure Efforts Shaped the American Civil War.* Nashville: Rutledge Hill Press, 2002

Jones, Rev. J. William, D.D. *Southern Historical Society Papers,* volume X. Millwood N.Y.: Kraus Reprint Co., 1977

Klein, Maury, *Edward Porter Alexander.* Athens: University of Georgia Press, 1971.

Knetsch, Joe, *Florida's Seminole Wars, 1817-1858.* Charleston, S.C.: Arcadia Publishing, 2003.

Kross, Gary, "July 3rd Action at Culp's Hill, Pickett's Charge," *Blue & Gray Magazine*, volume XVI, number 5 (June 1999).

Lamb, William. *The Life and Times of Col. William Lamb, 1835-1909*. Austin, Texas: privately published, 2000

Lee, Lawrence. *The History of Brunswick County, North Carolina*.

Lee, Lawrence. Unpublished manuscript in the collection of the author.

Lee, Susan P., *Memoirs of William Nelson Pendleton, D.D.*. Harrisonburg, Va.: Sprinkle Publications, 1991

Linn, Jo White, Private Manuscript, Salisbury, N.C., April 1994

Longacre, Edward G., *The Man Behind the Guns, A Military Biography of General Henry J. Hunt, Commander of Artillery, Army of the Potomac*. Cambridge, Mass.: Da Capo Press, 2003.

Marvel, William, *Lee's Last Retreat, the Flight to Appomattox*. Chapel Hill: University of North Carolina Press, 2002.

The Messenger, Wilmington, N.C.

Military Historical Society of Massachusetts, *Papers of the Military Historical Society of Massachusetts*, volume IX. Wilmington, N.C.: Broadfoot Publishing Company, 1989.

Moore, Mark A., *The Wilmington Campaign and the Battles for Fort Fisher*. Campbell, California: Savas Publishing Company, 1999.

Moore, Robert H., *The 1st and 2nd Stuart Horse Artillery. The Virginia Regimental Histories Series*. Lynchburg, Va.: H. E. Howard, Inc., 1985.

The Morning Star News, Wilmington, N.C.

Murray, R. L., *E. P. Alexander and the Artillery Action in the Peach Orchard*. Wolcott, N.Y.: Benedum Books, 2000.

New York Daily News, March 13, 1865.

Patterson, Lorrie. *Our Lady of the Snow Bulletin*. February, March, 1954.

Pfanz, Harry W., *The Battle of Gettysburg*. Ft. Washington, Pa.: Eastern National Park and Monument Association, 1994

Pfanz, Harry W., *Gettysburg, The Second Day*. Chapel Hill: University of North Carolina Press, 1987.

Priest, John Michael, *Antietam, The Soldiers' Battle*. New York: Oxford University Press, 1989.

Ramsay, John A., *John Andrew Ramsay Papers, 1852-1900*, Southern Historical Collection, Wilson Library, University of North Carolina, Chapel Hill.

Reaves, Bill, compiled by. *Reaves Collection*, series I, volume 61, arranged by J. K. Davis, Jr., New Hanover County Public Library, Wilmington, N.C.

Reilly, James, "Account of Fall of Fort Fisher," manuscript in William L. DeRosset Paper, 1862-1904, North Carolina State Archives, Raleigh.

Rohrer, Mrs. Pat Doerner. Family Letters.

Rollins, Richard, "Confederate Artillery at Gettysburg: The Plan," *North & South Magazine*, volume 2, number 7 (September 1999).

Rollins, Richard, "The Failure of Confederate Artillery in Pickett's Charge," *North & South Magazine*, volume 3, number 4 (April 2000).

Salisbury Post, Salisbury, N.C., January 28, 1909, September 2, 1945.

Scarborough, Franklin, Undated clipping on Stoneman's Raid from the *Salisbury Post*, Salibury, N.C.

Simpson, Col. H. B., *Hood's Texas Brigade, Lee's Grenadier Guard*. Hillsboro, Texas: Hill Junior College Press, 1977.

Simpson, Colonel Harold B., *Gaines Mill to Appomattox, Waco and McLennan County in Hood's Texas Brigade*. Waco, Texas: Texian Press, 1988.

Sprunt, James. *Chronicles of the Cape Fear River, 1660-1916*. Raleigh, N.C.: Edwards & Broughton Printing Co., 1916.

Storrick, W. C., *Gettysburg, Battle and Battlefield*. N.Y.: Barnes & Noble Books, 1994.

Strother, David H. *Second Manassas*. N.Y.: Time-Life Books, 1995.

Thomas, John Peyre, *The History of the South Carolina Military Academy*. Charleston: Walker, Evans & Cogswell Co., Publishers, 1893.

Walkley, Stephen, *History of the Seventh Connecticut Volunteer Infantry—Hawley's Brigade, Terry's Division, Tenth Army Corps, 1861-1865*, Southington, Connecticut: privately published, 1905.

The War of the Rebellion, Official Records of the Union and Confederate Armies, Washington, D.C.: Government Printing Office, 1880-1901.

Wert, Jeffry D. *General James Longstreet, the Confederacy's Most Controversial Soldier*. N.Y.: Simon & Schuster, 1994.

Wert, Jeffey D., *Gettysburg, Day Three*. N.Y.: Simon & Schuster, 2001.

Wilcox, Arthur M. and Warren Ripley, *The Civil War at Charleston*. Eighteenth edition, Charleston: The News and Courier and The Evening Post, 1994.

The Wilmington News, Wilmington, NC.

The Wilmington Star, Wilmington, NC, September 30, 1868; May 23, 1869; July 27, 1893.

Wilmington Morning Star News, Wilmington, NC, June 16, 1893; December 1891; June 14-16, 1893

Wilmington Weekly Star, Wilmington, NC, November 3, 1893.

Wise, Jennings Cropper, *The Long Arm of Lee, The History of the Artillery of the Army of Northern Virginia. Lincoln*. University of Nebraska Press, 1991

INDEX

Archer guns, 32

Arendell, Thomas, 162-163

Armistice Day, 187

Armstrong rifled gun, 152

Army of the James, 134-135, 153

Army of Northern Virginia, 24-25, 33, 35, 39, 40-41, 44-45, 48, 52-53, 55-60, 63-64, 67-68, 70-71, 73, 113-115, 117, 119-121, 126-128, 131-133, 135-138, 142, 175-178, 183, 185, 191

Army of the Potomac, 45, 59-60, 68-69, 115, 117, 119, 126-128, 134, 142, 180

Army of Tennessee, 64, 134

Ashland, 34

Associated Railways of the Carolinas, 167

Athlone, Ireland, 11-12, 194

Avezzana, General, 167

Bachman, W. K., 45, 51

Bachman's Battery, 124

Bacon, Jr., Henry, 187

Badhaim, Jr., William, 146

Bahama Islands, 146

Baker, Captain W. B., 162

Baldwin, Briscoe G., 137-138

Baldwin, Florida, 168

"Baldy" (horse), 115

Ballsville, Virginia, 176

Ballydonagh, Ireland, 11

Baltimore crossroads, 32

Baltimore, Maryland, 113

Barry, Captain John, 194

Barry, John Decatur, 69

Bartlett, Joseph J., 178-179

Batteries I and K, First Ohio Artillery, 65

Battery A, 13-15

Battery Buchanan, 153-154, 156, 158-160, 162 -164, 167, 169, 192

Battery C, Sumter, Georgia Artillery, 11th Battalion of Light Artillery, 67

Artillery, 11th Battalion Light Artillery, 49

Bell, Louis, 154-155
Bell's Union Brigade, 157
Bellona cannon, 61, 118
Bellona rifled guns, 32, 35
Bellona Iron Works, 32
Bellona, Virginia, 176
Benjamin, Judah P., 168
Benjamin, Mrs. Rosa, 23
Benning's Georgia Brigade, 118
Bermuda, 146, 168
Big Cypress Swamp, 17
Big Round Top, 113
Bigelow's Battery, 118
"Bill" (horse), 117, 125
Billups, Turner, 137
Billy Bowlegs, 17
"bit of woods, the," 122
Black Horse Tavern, 116
Black, Calvin M., 23
Blackwater River, 68
Blakely guns, 31, 64
Blandford Church, 140
Block House,
Bloody Angle, 137
Blount, Captain, 71
Bolles, J., 167
Boonsborough, 56, 75
Boswell, James Keith, 39-40
Bowers, Mr., 169
Braddock Road, 28
Braddy, Kinchen J., 162
Braddy's Battery, 162
Bragg, Braxton, 15, 151, 153-155
Branch, John Luther, 19
Brandy Station, Virginia, 132
Brazos Santiago, 13
Breathed, James, 121

Cleveland, Mrs. Grover (Frances Folsom), 191-192

Cleveland, Grover, 191-192

Cobham's Depot, 133

Cockpit Point (Possum Nose), 28

Coddle Creek Settlement, 22

Coehorn mortars, 140-141

Coffee mill guns (machine guns), 35

Cold Harbor, 137

Colored Troops, United States, 80-81

Columbia, South Carolina, 179

Columbiad siege guns, 149, 154

Columbus County, North Carolina, 189

Committee on the Conduct of the War, 119

Communication, 69

Company A, Tenth Regiment, North Carolina State Troops, 10, 21

Company B, Third Battalion, Light Artillery, 146

Company C, Confederate States Marines, 99

Company C, Third Battalion, North Carolina Light Artillery, 99

Company D, First Battalion North Carolina Heavy Artillery, 162

Company D, Thirteenth North Carolina Battalion, 148, 164

Company D, Thirteenth Battery, North Carolina Light Artillery, 100

Company F, Tenth North Carolina, 162

Company G, Seventh Connecticut, 160

Company H, Second United States Artillery, 12-13

Company K, Tenth North Carolina, 148, 153, 162-163

Company L, Twenty-First South Carolina, 162

Confederate Avenue, 122

Confederate Conscription Act of 1862, 74

Confederate First National Flag, 23

Confederate Marine Corps, 167

Confederate Medical Director's Office, 132

Confederate States Convention, 20

Confederate States Marines, 99-100, 103

Confederate Veterans Association, 187

Confederate War Department, 39

Congressional Committee on the Conduct of the War, 171

Cooper, Samuel, 151

Corran, Patrick, 14
Cotton, 48
County Westmeath, 11
Craig's Landing, 154
Crater, the, 141
Crook, George, 134
C.S.S. Georgia, 168
C.S.S. Sumter, 168
Cullen, D'Orsay, 73
Culpeper, 119
Culpeper Court House, 70, 131
Culp's Hill, 115, 118, 120
Curran Farm, 116
Custer, George A., 179-180
Curtis, Newton Martin, 150-151, 154-156, 171
Cushing, Alonzo H., 125
Cushing's Battery, 126
Custer, George A., 113-114
C. W. Yates and Company, 193

Dahlgren Howitzers, 15, 27, 53, 66
Dahlgren, John A., 53
Dahlgren, Madeline Vinton, 53
Dahlgren, Captain Ulric, 119
Darby, Elizabeth, 192
Dardingkiller, Sergeant Frederick, 19-20
Davies, Jr., Henry E., 177
Davis & Wiley Bank, Salisbury, North Carolina, 186
Davis, Eliza, 167
Davis, Jefferson, 15, 20-21, 25-26, 33, 38-39, 51, 66, 70, 74, 119, 131, 151,
    167-168, 175, 186
Davis, Joseph, 167
Dearing, James, 70-71, 128
Deatonville, 177
Dennen, Father Christopher, 191, 194
Department of North Carolina, 44, 151
Department of North Carolina and Southern Virginia, 132

General Hospital Number 4, 139
General Order Number 28, 148
General Order Number 61, 69
General Pickett's Line, 82
Georgetown, South Carolina, 191
Georgia Brigade, 63
"German" Charleston Artillery, 51
Gettysburg, 114-116, 127, 131-132, 180
Gerrysburg Campaign, 132
"ghost train", 123, 126
Gibbes, Major, 179-180
"Gibraltar of the South, The" 145
Gordon, John B., 175
Gordonsville, 34, 133, 135
Governor Chase, 170
Governor's Island, New York, 170, 172
"Granny Lee", 33
Grant, Ulysses S., 61, 134-135, 137-138, 142, 148, 151-152, 175, 178-179
"Gray Eagle" (horse), 115
Great Seal of the Confederacy, 104
"Great Yankee Skedaddle," 27, 69
Great Snowball Fight of 1863, 63
Green, C.A., 63
Greencastle, Pennsylvania, 70, 119
Greenville, North Carolina, 67
Greenwood Cemetery, New York City, 173
Greenwood, 115
Griffin, William H., 121
Guidon Hall, 46
Guilford Battleground Celebration, 186
Guinea Station, 65, 69

Hagerstown, Maryland, 113, 128
Hagood, Johnson, 154-155
Halifax, 168
Hall, D. Josephus W. home, Salisbury, North Carolina, 187
Hall, Guidon, 30

Hampton, Lucy, 179
Hampton, Sarah "Sally," 179
Hampton, Wade, 179
Hampton Roads, Virginia, 147, 151-153
Hanaway, Ephriam, 113
Hancock, Winfield Scott, 67, 75-76, 117, 124, 135
Hanover Junction, 34, 43, 137
Hardister, Jonathan, 37
Harper's Ferry, 56-57
Harris Granite Company, 187
Harrison's Landing, 36-37
Harvie, Colonel Edwin J., 59
Haskell, John Cheves, 64, 67-68, 71, 73, 118, 131, 137-138, 140-142, 165, 177-179
Haskell's Battalion, 131, 133, 136, 140-142, 176-178
Hassell, William, 101
Haupt, Herman, 127
Haw's Shop, 137
Haynesworth, Cadet George E., 19
Hazel River, 43
Hazlett, Charles E., 61, 67, 117-118
Haxlett's Battery, 124
Hebert, Louis, 164
Hedrick, John J., 20
Henry family, 189, 191
Henry, Anna Jane, 189, 193
Henry, Major Winston, 71, 73, 118, 131
Henry, Madge, 189, 193
Henry, Martha E. (Reilly), 189, 193
Henry, Mathias Winston, 64
Henry P. Matthews house, 47
Henry, William R., 189, 191
Henry, William Raphael, 191
Henry's Battalion, 115, 121
Henry's Battery of the First Corps, 59
Herring family, 191
Heth, Henry, 114

Periostitis, 139

Perry House, 136

Petersburg, Virginia, 67, 70, 138-142, 167, 175-176

Petersburg and City Point Railroad, 138

Petersburg and Weldon Railroad, 138

Petersburg Railroad, 65

Pettigrew, James J., 121

Phillips, Lewis Guy (Her Majesty's Grenadier Guards), 65

Phillips's Battery, 118

Pickett, George E., 121-123, 138

Pickett's Division, 124

Pickett's (General) Line, 143

Pickett-Pettigrew Charge, 124, 126, 128

Pimlico River, 67

Pipe Creek Line, 115, 117

Pitman, James M., 56

Plank Farm, 116

Pleasants, Henry, 140

Pleasonton, Alfred, 120, 124

Plymouth, North Carolina, 128

Point Lookout, Maryland (prison camp), 137

Polk, James K., 13

Pope, John, 29-30, 32, 34, 42, 45, 47, 51, 60

Port Isabel, Texas, 13

Porter, Commodore David, 147

Porter, Rear Admiral David Dixon, 147-148, 151-155

Potomac River, 28, 51-52, 57-58, 70, 114, 128, 132

"powder vessel," 148, 171

Powell, John R., 163-164

Powhatan Court House, Virginia, 176

Prayer (spirituality), 57, 86

Presbyerian, 23

Prime, Major, 172

Prospect Hill, 62

Prostitution, 65

Puebla, 13

"Pulpit," the (hospital), 157-158

13362277R00123

Made in the USA
Charleston, SC
04 July 2012